Addiction - This being human
A New Perspective

by
Ronnie Aaronson

authorHOUSE®

AuthorHouse™
1663 Liberty Drive
Bloomington, IN 47403
www.authorhouse.com
Phone: 1-800-839-8640

© 2013 Ronnie Aaronson. All rights reserved.

No part of this book may be reproduced, stored in
a retrieval system, or transmitted by any means
without the written permission of the author.

Published by AuthorHouse 2/19/2013

ISBN: 978-1-4259-6045-2 (sc)
ISBN: 978-1-4670-1239-3 (e)

Any people depicted in stock imagery provided by Thinkstock are models,
and such images are being used for illustrative purposes only.
Certain stock imagery © Thinkstock.

Because of the dynamic nature of the Internet, any web addresses or
links contained in this book may have changed since publication and
may no longer be valid. The views expressed in this work are solely those
of the author and do not necessarily reflect the views of the publisher,
and the publisher hereby disclaims any responsibility for them.

This being human is a guest house.
Every morning a new arrival.

A joy, a depression, a meanness,
Some momentary awareness comes
As an unexpected visitor.

Welcome and entertain them all!
Even if they're a crowd of sorrows,
Who violently sweep your house
Empty of its furniture,
Still,
Treat each guest honourably.
He may be clearing you out for some new delight.

The dark thought, the shame, the malice,
Meet them at the door laughing
And invite them in.

Be grateful for whoever comes,
Because each has been sent
As a guide from beyond.

-Rumi

TABLE OF CONTENTS

ACKNOWLEDGEMENTS ix

PREFACE xi

INTRODUCTION xv

Chapter 1   THE SELF-CARE AND SELF-HARM CONTINUUM. 1

Chapter 2   OUR PLACE ON THE CONTINUUM – Part One – 11

Chapter 3   OUR PLACE ON THE CONTINUUM – Part Two – 25

Chapter 4   OUR STATE OF MIND 37

Chapter 5   OUR BODY STORY-LINES AND MEMORY 51

Chapter 6   OUR SHAME PROCESS 65

Chapter 7   KEVIN'S STORY 89

Chapter 8	MICHELLE' STORY	109
Chapter 9	THIS BEING HUMAN	141
REFERENCES		155
INDEX		165

ACKNOWLEDGEMENTS

I would like to thank Sarah House for working with me to set up the SWAN Project and Alison Scrivens and Hannah Duncan, in particular, for helping to keep the dream going.

Appreciation also to all my colleagues who gave me their encouragement and all the clients who agreed to have their stories included in this text especially Kevin and Michelle.

I would like to particularly thank my son Simon Richardson and my friend Morris Kapatula for their valuable comments and unending gratitude to my god-daughter Hannah Pearce and Yuki Williamson for all the editing hours they have endured.

Words fail me to express the amount of support offered by, and the amount of gratitude due to Robin, my husband, who has supported me in all areas of my life including the writing of this book.

I would like this edition of the book to be dedicated to my children Simon Richardson, Anna Boulger, Tom Richardson, Matthew Aaronson and Lily Boulger, my first grandchild and to the many other grandchildren that I hope may follow.

PREFACE

> All our heart's courage is the
> echoing response to the
> first call of Being which
> gathers our thinking into the
> play of the world.
> ~Martin Heidegger

The conscious impetus for writing this book, which I had been meaning to do for a while, was to share the theoretical base on which the SWAN Project in Bristol was founded for the many students who do their placement with us. The project was set up to help anyone in recovery from alcohol abuse and was based on psychotherapeutic principles and theories. The trigger which fired me with passion to write at a particular moment was an incident that happened to one of our clients. Andrea reported how she had been mugged. The police had been patrolling nearby and came to her aid and were very interested until she mentioned that her methadone had been stolen and then they walked off. It struck me yet again that the chaos and harm that results from addiction is often seen as self-inflicted. While this is true at one level, the lack of choice about drinking or using drugs once the addiction has a hold on the individual means it is not true at another level. By writing this book for a wider audience, I hoped to bring more understanding and therefore engender more compassion. My hope is that this book will at least prompt discussion around the issues presented here.

Once I started writing, it was as if myriad streams of thought and feeling held in my body joined to form a river with such power that I could not ignore them until the words were out. At this point I realised that these outpourings were an attempt to share my own journey and reflect upon how I discovered my own self-compassion, which has been nurtured by understanding and relating my experience to psychotherapy theory. I hope in explaining some of the theories here, I might inspire others to gain a more compassionate perspective on their and other's lives.

My own life experience has been enriched by contact with others, many of whom have sought me out because their lives had become unmanageable due to excessive alcohol use. These words are dedicated to each one. This small volume is my attempt to normalise and humanise addictive behaviour. Too many individuals who come for help relate events where they have not been treated with respect because of their addiction, even if they were trying to control, or reduce their alcohol intake or were on a reducing methadone script at the time.

Although much of my working life has been spent working with those who are having problems of varying severity with alcohol, I hope that the theories illuminated in this volume will be useful for thinking about addictions in general.

I would like readers to hold in mind that the theories presented are only that; they are not proven hypothesis or fact. If they resonate with your body or your experience, you will be more likely to identify with them and hold them as truth. What is ultimately true, however, is that we are all unique individuals who share our human being-ness. Likewise, our experiences of the world, though different from each other, will sit somewhere on the continuums of pain/pleasure, not-good-enough-mothering/too-good-mothering, excessively shamed/not shamed, excessive use of mood-altering substances/little use of mood-altering substances and self-harm/self-care. I am aware that I have had to generalise as I have been able to portray only particular slices of these continuums.

I have made several conscious decisions about how I present these words, keeping in mind how I would like them to be received. I have chosen to keep the word 'client' to a minimum as some professionals working in the field work with 'service users' or 'patients' and it is easy to disengage from the written word if the terminology is jarring with a reader's routine language. I have tried deliberately to use phrases which are *less* dispassionate than 'client' and 'service user' in order to help the reader to think of this client group as individuals, all with their own unique stories and difficulties. To the same end, I have also chosen to include some vignettes, with the permission of each person, so as to include more personal stories and bring the narrative alive.

I have kept to a few themes, rather than included all psychotherapy theory that could be useful when working with addiction, so as not to dilute the impact and confuse anyone for whom these ideas are new or less familiar. By using as little jargon as possible and keeping the language plain, I sought to make these ideas accessible to as large an audience as possible. Jargon and clinical terms can also keep us in our heads, dissociating us from our feelings, and since I am writing about people who use substances to distance themselves from their emotions and physical sensations, I did not want this book to parallel that process.

This is not intended to be an academic piece of work but rather a passionate plea for more understanding and compassion for this client group. I have referenced some authors in the text, but others are only alluded to and these sources appear in the bibliography.

This short volume is offered as a taste of a delicious meal that is on offer, so at the end of each chapter I have suggested further reading for those who might wish to delve deeper. With the exception of Melanie Klein's book, I have chosen those that are more readable. However, I have included her book because, if you can make sense of it, it is extremely rich. A full bibliography is also provided at the back of the book.

INTRODUCTION

> He looked at his own soul
> with a Telescope. What seemed
> all irregular, he saw and
> shewed to be beautiful
> Constellations.
> ~Coleridge

As we listen, try to understand and think theoretically about another person's inner world, so our way of being with them is subtly changed, maybe in the way we hold our body, change our facial expression, or use the tone of our voice. Whatever the change is, the person notices it on an unconscious level. They can detect that something has shifted in our thinking about them. They seem to know intuitively that now is the time to make a disclosure that they had previously been hanging on to, for example. The ever-changing way in which we think about a particular person, as our work progresses, has a substantial impact on the relationship.

Professionals who work with individuals showing addictive behaviour will have a particularly wide variety of ways of being with their clients because there are so many conflicting physiological, behavioural and psychological theories about the roots of addiction which one we hold will affect the way in which we perceive these people.

Historically, treatment for the majority of clients who misuse chemical substances has been split off from psychotherapy, for two main reasons. First, psychoanalytic psychotherapy was not found to be helpful with this client group, even if the individual seeking help was dry or clean. Secondly, a process called the Twelve Steps devised by the founders of Alcoholics Anonymous, in keeping with their own experience of recovery, did help large numbers of people to become and stay abstinent. The failure of psychoanalytic psychotherapy, and the success of AA, together with its offshoots like Narcotics Anonymous at least partially explain why treatment for substance abuse has developed mainly outside the arena of psychotherapy. Due to what has been seen as the exclusive success of the Twelve Step Programme, a personal experience of an addiction has been seen as a prerequisite for professionals working in the addictions field and, until recently, counselling and psychotherapy training was a qualification rarely considered particularly relevant.

Psychoanalytic psychotherapy proved unproductive with this client group for several reasons. Following Freud's pioneering work early analysts believed that their patient's difficulties were mainly to do with internal conflicts between unconscious wishes and fears. Freud recommended that the analyst should not allow his own personality to intrude in the treatment. Part of the analyst's task, as he saw it, was to be as unobtrusive as possible. He suggested that if analysts provided a blank screen, the patients would respond to the analyst from their unconscious wishes and fears. These could then be explored and would thus become less potent and facilitate behaviour change.

This blank screen technique encourages the transference relationship to emerge, where a client tries to make sense of the unknown aspects of the analyst. The transference relationship can be seen as the process by which we transfer our experience of past relationships, our emotions, our thoughts and our expectations, on to our present relationships. For example, if John has experienced abandonment in his first relationship, he will enter other relationships with the fear, at some level, of being abandoned. He will unconsciously notice and interpret actions and comments made by Jill in the light of this fear. As evidence gathers that John is about to be abandoned he might act in a way which leads him either to abandon Jill before she abandons him, or push her into leaving him. In this way the expectation is confirmed. Of course, thoughts about leaving the relationship may not have been initially real for Jill, but she might become confused, or start to have thoughts about leaving the relationship as she picks up these abandonment feelings from John. This transfer of our experience from the past to the present is the body/mind's attempt to keep us safe. For example, if we have a bad car accident, the next time we need to travel by car we may have an emotional response that is fearful. The body/mind tries to protect us from further physical injury. In relationships the body/mind also tries to help us to avoid pain - emotional pain. Psychoanalytic psychotherapy today still works largely with this transference relationship.

Research indicates that substance abuse is positively correlated with physical, emotional and sexual abuse and neglect (Miller et al (1993), Widom (1994), Wilsnack et al (1997), Paul E Mullen and Jillian Fleming (1998)). In individual cases where this is true, it is possible that a transference relationship with the therapist is likely to be experienced as abusive if it is not talked through and explored in a compassionate, non-withholding way. The blank screen in psychoanalytic psychotherapy has the potential to mirror the initial destructive relationship. Much of this client group's unhelpful early learning, as a victim of abuse or neglect, would have been about the inability to have an impact on another in relationship and the individual's early experience might be confirmed and reinforced by the analyst's silence in traditional psychoanalytic psychotherapy.

These early analysts believed that, for the patient to fully engage with the analytic process optimal frustration was needed. They saw the energy that arose from frustration as essential to the process. To this end, analysts did not respond to their patients' interactions. Anxiety levels are usually high in people who seek help with alcohol and so to raise their frustration and anxiety levels further would not be helpful. In fact, given that individuals use substances to cope with their emotional difficulties, it is probable that raising levels of frustration or anxiety would provoke further drinking or drug taking.

Humanistic psychotherapy, with its emphasis on the real and the reparative relationship, offers a very different 'way of being' with the client. Sadly, it has taken longer to be recognised and to be seen as effective as its psychoanalytic counterpart. Gelso and Carter (1985) have described what happens in the real relationship as follows:

> "One's perceptions and interpretations of another's behaviour are appropriate and realistic, the feelings are genuine, and the behaviour is congruent." (p186)

The relationship is based on meeting the client where they are in the present moment, in the belief that the client will thrive if the therapist provides a non-judgmental space and is able to respect them, be compassionate towards them and interact with them in a genuine way. In this way humanistic psychotherapy provides a reparative relationship, which Clarkson (1995) describes thus:

> "(The) intentional provision by the therapist of a corrective, reparative, or replenishing relationship

or action where the original parenting was deficient, abusive or over-protective." (p108)

It is true that person-centred counselling skills, which sit within the same framework of humanistic psychotherapy, have been recognised and are used in the treatment of substance misuse. As a result, many professionals working with addicted people are aware of the need to show unconditional positive regard, to be empathic and congruent with their clients in order to see them grow. However, these three core conditions are sometimes the *only* aspect of psychotherapy theory which informs the practise of many people working in this field.

Although a psychoanalytic way of being with the patient is not useful for this particular client group, some of the theory it has to offer is very relevant and helpful. Particular theories have helped me to think about and work with individuals who have been using mood-altering drugs to cope with their emotional upset and I would like to offer a commentary on them in this context. I have included theories from different schools of psychotherapy on the basis that they help illuminate some aspect of substance misuse. Here follows a short commentary on each to whet the appetite.

Turp's (2003) work on self-harm normalises self-harming activities. She sees self-harming activities as a behaviour that many of us use to deal with unmanageable emotions and points out that the severity of the self-harming activity is related to the amount of unmanageable emotional distress we feel. I look at this in relation to drinking excessive amounts of alcohol and/or taking hard drugs. In order to consider why some of us experience so much emotional difficulty for so much of the time, I have included the notion of transference and the Parent/Adult/Child model provided by Transactional Analysis.

Other ideas that go towards explaining why some of us have trouble coping with our emotional difficulties are Winnicott's (1960) concept of 'good- enough mothering' and Bion's (1962) concept of 'the container' and 'the contained'. Those of us who use a substance to cope with our emotional difficulties have not generally experienced good-enough emotional care as infants and so have not had the opportunity to internalise a model which can help us to deal with the emotional ups and downs of every day life.

The work of Melanie Klein (1946), Karpman (1968) and Berne (1970) have been included because they offer insights into a state of mind particularly relevant to this client group. The victim state of mind seems to resonate with many individuals using substances to cope, possibly because of the often helpless situations in which they found themselves during childhood or at some other point in their lives.

Reich (1947) helps us to think about the impact that our experience has on our body and the defences the body uses. These defences, if used regularly, can become frozen in our bodies and can cut us of from our emotional life - both painful and joyous experiences - leaving us with little sense of self; of who we are; how we feel; what we want from life.

Shame plays a large part in the lives of those with an addictive life-style. Understanding shame, its origins, its effect on relationships and how it may be played out can help people to end the addictive cycle. If shame and counter-transference are not understood by professionals working with this client group, they could be pulled into a shaming relationship. Gilbert and Proctor (2005) have highlighted the impact that shame has on the ability of clients to hear positive feedback. Positive remarks and affirmations cannot nourish if they cannot be taken in, in the same way that medicine would not work if we were unable to assimilate it. Defences and resistance can arise when our concept of self is challenged, even when the challenge is positive.

In each case I look at the implications of the theories presented in terms of how we might perceive and be, in a compassionate way, with individuals who come for help with addictive behaviour. I likewise comment on how we might work more productively with the often redundant and debilitating defences evident in the narratives, breathing patterns, body story lines and the body/mind split commonly present in people sustaining an addiction.

Two case studies provide concrete examples of the different threads I have chosen to highlight. I hope that this will give the reader a better feel for how they might all join together in a tapestry.

Finally, I offer suggestions about how counselling and psychotherapy theory can help us work with those who come for help and how counselling can provide a reparative relationship, one that could help individuals to develop a stronger sense of who they are; be in touch with and understand their feelings, know what their needs are and have the sense that they can fulfil them.

Further reading:

BATEMAN A. & HOLMES J. (1995) *Introduction to Psychoanalysis*. London: Routledge.

KAHN M. (2001) *Between Therapist and Client*. NY: Henry Holt and Co.

1

THE SELF-CARE AND SELF-HARM CONTINUUM.

> Self-harm is "a purposeful, if morbid, act of self-help"
> -Favazza (1989, quoted in Turp)

When the term 'self-harm' is used in relation to substance abuse it refers to the deliberate act of consuming an excessive amount of a mood-altering drug, despite the knowledge that it will result in physical self-injury. The act of drinking, smoking, sniffing or injecting a drug is seen as purposeful and intentional. So these acts often provoke strong emotional and critical responses from others. The question that is not often considered is what purpose and intention these acts serve.

Turp (2003) understands general self-harm as an umbrella term for behaviour;

> "1) that results, whether by commission or omission, in avoidable physical self-harm and 2) that breaches the limits of acceptable behaviour, as they apply at the place and time of enactment, and hence elicit a strong emotional response." (p36)

As a term, self-harm usually describes behaviour confined to a small group of people who deliberately abuse their own bodies. When used generally it refers to anyone intentionally harming himself/herself although most commonly it refers to cutting or some other form of self-maiming.

Turp calls this view of self-harm the "qualitative leap model of self-harm". She challenges the view that the behaviour of people who self-harm is seen as different from that of 'normal' people, and proposes in its place a continuum model of self-harm. The latter presents self-harming activities on a continuum from "good-enough self-care" to "compromised self-care" to "mild self-harm" to "moderate self-harm" and finally to "severe self-harm". Turp points out that most of us exist somewhere along this line, so that self-harming behaviour becomes normalised. She notes that some of these activities are culturally acceptable, whereas others are not. She uses the acronym CASHA to distinguish "culturally accepted self-harming acts or activities".

Whether these activities are acceptable or not seem to be more a question of how much they impact on others' lives, rather than how dangerous they are to the individual. Patterns of acceptance change remarkably rapidly both in response to social fashion or evolving perceptions of risk. Smoking used to be acceptable, but became less acceptable as society became more aware of its indirect impact on others. By contrast, breaking the skin on your arm with a razor, although at one level is less harmful than smoking, is socially unacceptable because of the distress it imposes on the onlooker.

In terms of acceptability, mood altering drugs do not fit neatly into either the acceptable or unacceptable category. Whether it is acceptable or not depends partly on the quantity used and also on the perception of the person making the value judgement. It

Addiction - This being human

remains socially acceptable to drink in moderation, but people who drink to excess and go on to exhibit unsociable behaviour are shown an ever decreasing degree of tolerance. Excessive use of mood-altering drugs and anti-social behaviour are often closely linked. As a result, shame surrounds many aspects of drug and alcohol abuse. What is considered unacceptable behaviour also differs from social group to social group. For example, teenagers may find it abnormal not to take Ecstasy when out clubbing, whereas a group of social drinkers might become embarrassed or critical if one of their friends gets too intoxicated.

Once someone is physically addicted to a substance they will need to keep using that substance just to remain pain-free and feeling normal. Research has shown that the greatest reason given for self-harming activities is the 'relief of feelings' (Arnold, 1995, quoted in Turp, 2003), and yet there is a general assumption that is still prevalent which is that those abusing substances are choosing to self-harm. If however, we see alcohol and drug addiction as the result of someone managing their emotional and physical well-being in the best way they know how, we can be more compassionate towards them.

Most people start out as social drinkers or drug users. People who go on to become addicted to a substance are those who discover that it provides them with something beneficial. For example, a person may discover that they become more confident, less depressed, more fun to be with, less anxious, less bored, and so on when they drink or take a particular drug.

If we derive benefit from a particular behaviour, this information is stored in our memories so that the act and the satisfaction derived from it can be repeated. If we are using a chemical substance to deal with our anxiety, then there will be short-term benefits from drinking or taking drugs. This act will be stored in our body's memory as a 'good' way of being. The more often this happens, the stronger the link is made and the more difficult it will be for the individual to control their substance use in times of high stress, or anxiety. If the chosen form of dealing with emotional upset is to use an addictive substance, increasing amounts are needed in order to reach the same desired state. Weegmann (2003) makes the following comment:

> "The immediate manifestation of its use may be one or several of the following: an alteration in mood, a rising in self esteem, an increased vitality or energy, a sense of power or assertion, an intense affective experience or a nullifying of intense experiences, taking the edge off reality. Temporarily, therefore, the taking in of the drug can lead to a feeling of triumph over problems within the self, however this constitutes a pyrrhic victory." (p.36)

This battle, where the victor loses as much as he gains can be repeated endlessly because the effect of mood-altering substances easily confuses our brain in terms of cause and effect; the short-term consequences are perceived as beneficial and the link between ingestion and the long-term damaging effects are not experienced consciously. We might drink or use a drug to solve a particularly difficult situation and find that in the short-term the substance works. What we are less able to add to the equation is the long-term effect of that usage – the physical and psychological cost that accrues as we become more reliant on the chosen drug and become increasingly less able to cope with day-to-day issues.

Most people have a tendency towards some form of self-harm when their level of emotional upset becomes too much or unbearable. Some of us bite our nails, pick at our fingers, pull

Addiction - This being human

our hair, eat cakes, smoke cigarettes, drink coffee, cut our arms, exercise too vigorously, throw ourselves into work, drink or take drugs. My clinical experience indicates that in part our chosen method of self-harm depends on the severity of our physical or psychological distress. We adopt the behaviour that is at some level 'good-enough' to relieve the distress - no matter how temporarily. Often clients during the course of therapy will move from extreme to less severe levels of self-harm.

Fleur

When Fleur came to therapy she had a history of an eating disorder and using drugs and drink. She came to see me at a time when she had given up hard drugs and was struggling to stay abstinent from alcohol. As we worked together, the frequency of her lapses lessened as she learnt from each one.

The first lapse happened during a six-week break when Fleur had been away from home and therefore away from her regular support network; our project, her AA sponsor, friends and her AA meetings. It happened at a time when she had over-committed herself to support a group where she was a member. The actual trigger was conflict with another member of the group. Immediately after the incident, she drank a bottle of wine. She also had a few drinks over the following week. Reflecting on the incident later, Fleur was able to take on board the lack of support and the amount of stress she had put herself under.

Another lapse came after she walked out of our session at exactly the same time that a paramedic, who had attended to Fleur after one of her suicide attempts, left the adjacent room, having attended to someone else in the building. Fleur had an association between the ambulance crew, her various suicide attempts and being taken to a psychiatric ward. Even seeing an ambulance in the street brought up negative emotions in her body. This incident was more difficult for Fleur to cope with than the previous one so this time she drank two bottles of wine. She described it later as going onto "automatic pilot". Although her mind was telling her that this was "stupid" and "not going to help", it felt as if something stronger had propelled her toward the drinking.

As Fleur used alcohol less and less, she used other less severe self-harming acts. She would occasionally comb her head until she broke the scalp, forget to eat breakfast and lunch but then gorge on junk food when her blood sugar became so low that she found it difficult to think about anything else other than food, or forget to take her medication, and other similar things.

As time went on, Fleur learned to be in touch with her feelings, to understand them, to sit with them and manage them. Her difficult feelings stopped being acted out once she consciously experienced them. Although her lapses stopped, when Fleur became distressed she did sometimes resort to other self-harming behaviours, but they were less severe and less frequent.

These less severe forms of self-harm have been labelled 'hidden self-harm' by Turp. Although a high percentage of the population use hidden self-harming practices, they are rarely brought to the attention of professionals, because on the whole they do not disrupt every-day lives, whereas drug dependency often does. We can see that as Fleur is more able to contain her own emotions, her self-harming practices become more hidden and so more socially acceptable. Turp, comparing what is normally thought of as self-harm with CASHAs, comments:

> "There is a difference of intensity rather than one of kind. In other words, *the difference resides in the level of desperation and emotional distress involved.*" (p10)

Individuals may also sometimes have a felt sense about which particular form of self-harming behaviour will relieve a particular quality or essence of an emotional distress.

> Jane
>
> Jane had been to America to see her daughter. At the beginning of her flight home there was a thunderstorm and the plane was caught in turbulence. Being an anxious passenger, her fear grew and she felt as though she was about to be obliterated, even though her logic told her otherwise. She found the situation unbearable and to cope with her anxiety, in what seemed like a death-threatening situation, she drank excessively.
>
> On the same trip, Jane's partner had been expected to collect her from the airport at a particular time, but at the arranged time he did not appear. From experience she knew that he always phoned if he was going to be delayed. She had trouble trying to make sense of what had happened to him, other than the thought that he must have been involved in an accident. Her anxiety rose as she fantasised about life without him and she found herself pacing the terminal, eating chips, biscuits and a chocolate bar. This time food rather than alcohol provided the holding she needed.

When we talked through these incidents, we noted that in the first one her anxiety was for her own survival and in the second for another's. While trying to make sense of the two incidents, Jane realised that eating food on the plane would not have helped. When her partner was absent and longed for, digesting chips, biscuits and chocolate somehow helped her to feel that her partner was present: they filled an emptiness inside her. On the other hand, what was needed on the plane was not to fill a void, but to avoid being in the present moment. By drinking too much and not having to be present, she gained a sense of relief. She noted the irony that it was as if she had induced a sense of being obliterated by getting drunk, which was what she feared would happen if the plane crashed. It seems as if our unconscious provides the form of acting out that will alleviate that particular form of distress. We might exhibit different self-harming activities for different types or levels of anxiety.

These self-harming activities are something that we all have the capacity to do when our emotional arousal is greater than our capacity to deal with it. Being aware and remembering that this is normal human behaviour in circumstances when we are in pain, keeps to the forefront of our minds the pain and suffering that is being experienced by those acting it out. If self-harm in general can be seen as the acting out of emotional distress, then the gross self-harm, that which results from excessive use of chemical substances, reflects the severity and quality of the psychological distress.

It is easy to perceive excessive drinkers, or drug users, as manipulative and deliberately trying to deceive or offend us. This is not helpful to the therapeutic relationship. The 'dishonesty' which stems from denial needs to be seen in relation to the overpowering need of that individual to self-soothe in the only way they know how. Once we look at self-harming in this more general way it is more difficult to maintain a critical stance, and our compassion naturally opens towards individuals using substances.

Further reading:

TURP M. (2003) *Hidden self-harm. Narratives from Psychotherapy.* London: Jessica Kingsley Publishers Ltd

2

OUR PLACE ON THE CONTINUUM
– Part One –
– life's difficulties and our response to them –

*Fear is the cheapest room in the house
I would like to see you living in better conditions*
~Hafiz

*"The more you are able to honour and accept the
Now, the more you are free of pain, or suffering"*
~Eckhart Tolle

So, as we have seen, most of us use self-harming activities at times when we are particularly anxious or distressed. These behaviours exist on a continuum, with suicide at one end of the spectrum and hidden self-harming activities at the other. Where we sit on this particular continuum at any one time is related to the amount of emotional distress we are experiencing at the time. Individuals that use CASHAs have distress levels lower than those who use substances to cope.

Using an addictive substance to cope will commonly lead to an addictive habit. When we first come into recovery the habit often masks the triggers that initiated the substance use, but as we try to control their usage, the triggers re-emerge. To an onlooker, the kind of triggers that can set off a lapse might appear insignificant, for example, a row with a partner, missing a train or frustration at not being heard by an authority figure. It poses the question why these seemingly every-day events can trigger such high levels of self-harming behaviour. There are, of course, many contributory factors, some of them might be to do with the personal make-up of the individual, but theory provides us with answers that appear to apply to the majority of individuals using substances to cope with emotional difficulties.

From our knowledge of transference we know that present experience can trigger emotional feelings from the past. When our past experiences include trauma of some kind, we become hyper-vigilant and sensitive. We can re-experience overwhelming emotions that were encountered in the original traumatic situation, triggered by every-day events. Individuals who have suffered trauma at some point in their life sit further along the stress continuum because they experience events and situations as persecutory more easily. This heightened stress level will affect our frame of mind and our physiology.

The brain holds memories of painful experiences in an attempt to keep us safe. The more traumatic the remembered event, the more intense the future feelings of fear and anxiety will be when the memory is triggered. Transactional Analysis (Stewart, 1989) provides us with a model of self which includes three different, although overlapping, parts. These parts are referred to as ego states: different states from which we think, talk and act. Transactional Analysis refers to them as Parent, Adult and Child.

The Parent ego state refers to the ingrained voices which we have internalized from authority figures. It consists of conscious and unconscious recorded messages that get expressed in the 'self-talk' that goes on inside our heads. This self-talk can be very critical and might include phrases like 'under no circumstances', 'always' and 'you shouldn't'.

Our Child ego state can be described as our internal reaction, prompted by historical feelings, to current external events. When any emotional response is out of proportion to what is actually happening, this is a clue to the fact that we are being influenced by our past; we have regressed to our Child ego state. We are actually responding emotionally to something in the present *as though* it was the same as a previous experience. For example, a row with a partner might trigger emotions that originated in childhood, when a parental row, overseen and overheard, lead to the mother being beaten by the father. Missing a train might bring back emotional memories of feeling helpless and despairing at events in childhood; of being out of control and frustrated. Not being heard by an authority figure might re-activate feelings associated with our pain at not being heard by our parents.

Bell (1998) makes the point that seemingly trivial events can have a traumatizing effect on an individual because of the particular meaning they carry.

> Pat
>
> Pat was born into a dysfunctional and often violent household. She spent most of her early years in and out of foster homes or in care. Eventually she ended up in a children's home, where one of her carers sexually abused her. Whenever the abuse took place the perpetrator would bind her mouth with a red scarf. Pat came to associate red scarves with the abuse.
>
> For a long time afterwards, whenever she saw a red

> scarf, she would return to the feelings of helplessness and terror that she felt during the abuse, as the memories came back, even if she was in safe company and in a safe place at the time.

In contrast, when we are in our Adult ego stage we have the ability to feel, think and determine action in a logical way. We stay emotionally in the moment. As our Adult part experiences events in the present so our behaviour, even though it is coloured by our past experience, tends to be rational. When we experience events from our Child or Parent ego states, on the other hand, our past experience has the potential to dominate our behaviour. For example, if you have recently had a near drowning experience you might find it difficult to swim out of your depth, even though logic tells you that you are a strong swimmer. Just as Fleur drank to self-soothe even when she knew it was not what would help, when we feel threatened our behavior can be influenced by the unconscious memory of previous strategies that worked. Our logic is overridden by our unconscious mind's attempt to keep us safe.

When events can be generalised the memory of the connection between cause and effect is useful. For example, when we burn ourselves on an oven door, the association between the oven door and the burning sensation helps us not to repeat the damage to our skin when we next cook. However, in Pat's case the association with the red scarf was not useful as the experience could not be generalised: not everyone wearing a red scarf is going to act in an abusive way.

It may be useful to think of ourselves as being in the Child ego state when past emotions have been triggered in the present. It is often evidenced by our over-reaction to a situation. Once we can recognise this state, we can self-soothe by coming back into the present and looking at the situation, logically, from our Adult ego-state. In this way we can ground ourselves and reduce our anxiety levels.

Individuals who have suffered some form of abuse can be emotionally handicapped by the Parent ego-state. Excessive shame originates in an abusive power-laden relationship. We internalise authority figures whether they are positive or negative voices and so we have the potential to internalise a persecutory care-giver - the voice of the person who in the past shamed, abused or bullied us. Shame and self-criticism become entrenched processes when their repetition is extreme. Our Parent ego state can severely hinder us, if the authority figures that we have internalised have been abusive, or overly critical. If this is the case, it can provoke excessive amounts of self- criticism and self-punishment. We sometimes choose partners, or friends, who take on the same role as the abuser, or we can repeat the experience ourselves by keeping the abuser alive in our thoughts and by continuing to shame, abuse and bully *ourselves*. This will negatively affect our state of mind and keep our stress levels high.

Self-criticism, shame, dissociation, the capacity to self-soothe and self-harming behaviours are often inter-related. We know from research that self-criticism is significantly associated with the shame process (Gilbert and Miles, 2000). Constant self-criticism not only lowers our self-esteem, keeps us in a subservient frame of mind and damages our concept of self, but it also often reproduces the anger of the abusive other in the form of self-directed anger and hate. When self-hate and anger are present there is no place for feelings of self-compassion and self-love, without which the motivation and the ability to self-soothe is absent (Gilbert, 2000, Whelton and Greenberg, 2005). Healing starts as we begin to recognise that our critical or persecutory inner voices have little to do with how we are being perceived in the moment by others: when we can acknowledge that they are only a hollow echo from the past. The ability to have compassion for ourselves, to be self-accepting, understanding and forgiving develops from the experience of having had a loving, accepting, forgiving and compassionate care-giver.

Someone who has internalised an abusive other is doubly handicapped. First, they are lacking the caring voices and secondly, they have the burden of the critical or self-punishing voices. This stream of constant self-criticism will increase the intensity of our anxiety and stress levels. Even seemingly small amounts of anxiety can change our experience fundamentally. For example, if we are under threat of arriving late to an important meeting, we are less likely to stop for someone just approaching the zebra crossing. We are less able to be considerate of the other person or empathic and we might even experience the person wanting to cross the road as *deliberately trying to hinder us* and swear at them as we pass by. We might feel that this is not our usual behaviour, but it might be our normal behaviour when a low level of paranoia has been activated by the amount of stress present. Our perception of what is happening and our subsequent behaviour is influenced by our changed state of mind.

When we perceive that we are under threat, our fear system kicks in and can override our conscious wishes. This system is designed to activate a quick response to help us survive attack so in this state we respond to the environment in a fundamentally different way. When we perceive a threat and become fearful, as a consequence we become more vigilant, we react rather than respond, we are likely to jump to conclusions and overestimate the extent of the threat. Individuals can drink or inject a substance despite a conscious wish not to, when they perceive a physical or psychic threat. We often witness people in recovery lapsing when they are feeling threatened even though a large part of them does not want to drink or use. We all return to coping strategies that have worked in the past if we are feeling threatened to an overwhelming extent. There is no time to come up with a new strategy and it is too risky to rely on a new strategy which has not been tested under such extreme circumstances.

We can see then that our past experience impacts on our present emotional experience. It is true too that our current emotions are also affected by our past response to past emotions. The defences that we employ to deal with the overwhelming emotional experience of those traumatic events can themselves add further difficulties to our ability to cope with our emotional lives later on.

Often individuals have the fantasy that all they need to do is talk about a traumatic event in order to be cured. The notion corresponds to the idea that there is an instant solution, which of course is not the case. If they are too ready to disclose traumatic events before they have some ability to self-soothe, we, as therapists, need to stop them. When we have not had the experience of being in relationship with a trustworthy person, we tend to trust either everyone or no-one. The issue of trust needs to be talked through. Disclosing traumatic events immediately does not make for easy relationships outside the room. Inside the counselling room individuals need to have the ability to cope with the emotions that will be stirred up; they need to be able to ground themselves, before they start to look at the issues. If not, it is possible that these individuals can be re-traumatised and we collude with them in what could be seen at best as a lack of self-care, and at worst as a form of self-harm.

How trauma is experienced exists on a continuum as do the defences used against these emotional experiences: the greater the physical and emotional distress, the further the individual is likely to detach from it. We can see mild detachment at one end of the continuum and psychotic episodes at the other. Kepner (1993) explains what happens at a body level when a child is physically abused:

> "The child responds to such hurts by shrinking away from the contact surface of the skin and muscle. With repeated hurt, the child shrinks even further away from the source of pain, divorcing the sense of self from his or her body, disowning the location of pain to help reduce the damage." (p18)

While detaching from our painful body sensation is useful at the time of a trauma, it can result in a handicap: a more permanent detachment. Some individuals will distance themselves slightly from their emotions, while others, at the far end of the continuum, will dissociate completely. Davies and Frawley (1994) describe dissociation as:

> "the process of severing connections between categories of mental events –between the events that seem irreconcilably different, between actual events and their affective and emotional significance, between actual events and the awareness of their cognitive significance, and finally, as in the case of severe trauma, between the actual occurrence of real events and their permanent, symbolic, verbal mental representation."(p7)

Once a defensive strategy has worked for us, we tend to use the same defence in similar circumstances; for example, we might withdraw from contact with others whenever we feel overwhelmed and angry because this strategy worked well for us in our relationship with our parents. Emotions come in

Addiction - This being human

waves; they naturally build up gradually and then subside. So if we distance ourselves from our emotions, it is probable that we distance our contact at a relatively heightened state of the emotional discomfort and so do not experience the emotion subsiding. Subsequently, this makes it more difficult to stay in touch with the emotion, because we hold no memory of the emotion lessening. Similarly, if we have suppressed our emotions as a defence, we might only start to feel them when they have already reached an overwhelming level. For example, we do not feel frustration or irritation until it has built up into anger or rage.

When we disengage our feelings as an ongoing strategy, then what would have been a naturally passing emotion, or emotional process, might be held in the body, causing us difficulties because we have not been able to process it.

> Robert
>
> Robert's father died suddenly when he was studying for his A levels. Robert felt that he needed to keep going in order to pass his exams, so he did not engage with his grief, rather shelved it instead. Around the same time his mother's voice would occasionally start to crackle and Robert sometimes made fun of her in a good-humoured way. Shortly afterwards, his mother was diagnosed with throat cancer and died. Robert inherited his parents' house and became financially secure unexpectedly. Caught up in this whirlwind of events, Robert had no time to grieve for either of his parents as he became overwhelmed by a tangled mix of feelings: relief, sadness, guilt, gratitude, anger, regret and despair. He started to drink excessively.
>
> When he came to see us at the Swan Project he had

> been drinking heavily for about twelve years. He had been unable to mourn for his father or mother and the emotions were arrested in his body. Whenever he chose not to drink, the grief which he had not experienced, thought about or processed re-emerged. Counselling gave Robert the space and support that he needed to go through the grieving process which eventually rendered his need to drink alcohol to self-soothe redundant.

Once Robert understood that his past defence, which worked well to get him through his A levels had since then hampered his emotional well-being, he could be encouraged to re-engage with his emotions. It is useful to look at and review past defences and to consider whether they are still serving us. Once we are conscious of our past defences, we can choose to keep or to drop them.

The physical defence of distancing ourselves from our emotions has implications for how we think about what is happening. This thinking can be seen as a form of denial. We are able to deny the intensity, or even the existence, of the emotions involved. Again when these defences are repeatedly used, denial can become a strategy which can be frequently applied to all areas of an individual's existence, hampering their ability to perceive events clearly, even including positive achievements.

We need a language to think about and process our experience so if we have been brought up in a family where emotions are unacceptable and are kept hidden, we might lack the necessary emotional vocabulary. Similarly, if certain emotions have been unacceptable in our birth families an 'unacceptable' emotional response may be concealed by a more acceptable emotion. Ferster (1973) suggests, for example, that if the caregiver's response to anger from their child is to withdraw love,

Addiction - This being human

this child will replace what would have been his anger with anxiety. Initially he feels the anger, and because he knows it is unacceptable it either transmutes to shame due to the unacceptable nature of the emotion, or to anxiety about the potential withdrawal of support. Eventually this becomes a shorter loop and the child misses out on the feelings of anger and goes straight into the emotion of shame or anxiety.

It is interesting that our inner intelligence will often unconsciously find an outlet for what is being suppressed yet is needed. Tomkins (1963) notes that the state of intoxication that alcohol produces allows us to release suppressed emotions:

> "The smile of intimacy and tenderness, the look of excitement, sexual and otherwise, the unashamed crying of distress, the explosion of hostility, the intrusion of long suppressed terror, the open confession of shame, and the avowal of self-contempt." (p268)

If we have suppressed emotions, we have also suppressed what helps us to know, and have a sense of who we are: a sense of our emotional self. We might also feel attracted to others who display our suppressed emotion as we unconsciously feel the need to rely on that aspect of someone else. For example, if we have suppressed our anger, we might rely on someone else to hold our boundaries, and say "no" for us. This is one of the reasons why co-dependent relationships develop because we feel incomplete and inadequate to manage life on our own.

Dean

Dean's anger had been particularly volatile in relation to his parents during his teenage years. He recalled an incident when the family had been out visiting how on the way home in the car he and his father had a

> huge row. Dean asked his father to stop the car and he got out. After a long walk home, Dean found his father in tears. He was shocked. He had never seen his father cry before. Thereafter Dean suppressed his anger, without which Dean allowed others to take advantage of him. He drank when his resentment built up towards his friends and family and he felt unable to express his anger. It was difficult for Dean to see that he was allowing them to take advantage.

Dean talked this through with his therapist and came to understand how the same act of suppressing his anger, which had helped him to live in harmony with his parents during that period of his life, was now disabling him. Gradually, Dean was able to get back in touch with his anger and subsequently act on it in a productive way.

Often when a person who is not in touch with their anger talks about an incident which promotes anger, the angry feelings arise in the therapist. The anger is projected onto the therapist. If the anger is then disclosed by the therapist it can help the individual to take back the projection and start to integrate the feelings of anger. By the therapist disclosing what is happening for them physically and emotionally the emotion can be normalised, give vocabulary to the client and can give permission for the client to feel it. By reclaiming these split-off parts of ourselves and becoming a whole person, we lose the perceived need to rely on another and a tendency towards co-dependency.

If we have no understanding that a present situation can trigger past emotions and thoughts, and if we believe that our feelings are being aroused only in the present, the intensity of our emotions can appear to come upon us randomly. As we increasingly discover our historical emotional triggers we can begin to make more sense of what is happening to us in the present moment. Similarly if we know that when our fear system is activated, other bodily functions are temporarily put on hold while we deal with the threat including our logical thinking, then it becomes easier to make sense of what might otherwise seem like illogical behaviour.

Threat demands to be dealt with quickly. We can see that the so called 'immediate gratification' and the 'quick fix' of alcohol or drug use is a healthy response to an unhealthy situation, rather than the other way around. It is useful for individuals seeking help with addictive behaviour to understand why they become emotionally overwhelmed and that their reaction of 'instant gratification' is normal and healthy and not an 'insane' or 'stupid' act.

As we have seen, most people who use substances do so when their capacity to deal with their emotions is overwhelmed. This fact might be masked by a habit, but once the individual seeking help starts to cut back or stop using a substance, the triggers begin to become visible. We have looked at many reasons why individuals might feel overwhelmed. These include the recurring of previously uncontainable emotions by every-day situations, excessively critical internalised voices, redundant defences which are still in place, the lack of vocabulary and the experience of dealing with emotions generally. What seems to be essential, if sobriety is to be maintained, is that individuals are enabled to make sense of and to manage their emotions.

Further reading:

JACOBS M. (1986) *The Presenting Past*. Buckingham: Open University Press.

STEWART I. (1989) *Transactional Analysis Counselling in Action*. London: Sage.

3

OUR PLACE ON THE CONTINUUM
– Part Two –

– our capacity to cope –

> "To be held physically or emotionally by another human being gives us a sense that we are worthy of being cherished and loved. It fills us with a sense of safeness which allows us to take risks and grow."
> ~Fay Feltham

One hypothesis which has been put forward as to why some individuals feel more distress than others is that each of us has a different capacity to deal with emotional pain. It is probable that some of us have a higher tolerance threshold than others due to our genetic make-up, but there may be environmental reasons too. It has been proposed by Bion (1962) and Winnicott (1960) that our capacity to cope with emotional pain depends, at least in part, on the quality of the mothering that we received as infants.

To put forward their thinking Bion and Winnicott use the concepts of 'holding', 'containment', and the 'good-enough mother'. When we think of 'holding', we tend to think of physical holding, for example, as a mother might cradle her infant or perhaps an adult embrace, or even to support the weight of another. In whichever way we relate to the concept it is about physical contact. In psychotherapy when we refer to holding we are usually describing an emotional holding which also involves contact - *emotional* contact.

Bion recognised that a mother has the capacity to 'hold' her infant's distress. He identified the mother's calm state of mind as crucial for this holding, together with her capacity to listen to her infant's distressing communication, to make sense of it, process it and offer it back with a communication that is both congruent with the infant's emotional state and manageable for him.

For example, if a child cries with despair at having left a loved teddy bear somewhere, the 'holding' mother will empathise: "Oh, that's terrible, we've left teddy in the post office". The words are said in a tone which acknowledges the distress but does not key into the despair. "Never mind, we can put our coats on and quickly go to the post office and fetch him". Her voice becomes lighter. By acknowledging, bearing and then reducing the intensity of the emotion, she is able to transform the child's initial despair and he is able to process it in this state because it is no longer so intense.

Bion calls this process 'containment'. It is easy to imagine the mother's capacity to process emotion as a vessel and the child, as yet without any conscious awareness of his skin boundary, as a liquid. The mother is the 'container' and the infant's emotions are what she holds – what is 'contained'. Bion suggests that individuals that have had the experience of a primary carer who could manage their emotions are more likely to be able to manage their own emotions in adulthood.

Winnicott encourages our thinking along similar lines by

providing us with the concept of the 'good-enough' mother. The 'good-enough' mother is one who is in tune with her baby. She can intuitively read his emotional pain and knows what is needed to calm him down. These mothers have usually had 'good-enough' mothering themselves and Winnicott argues that it is these 'good-enough' mothers that are able to offer the most effective mothering to their infants.

He also identifies the 'not-good enough' mother and the 'too-good' mother. The 'not-good-enough' mother cannot attend to her child because she is usually caught up in her own emotional distress, e.g. a mother with a large number of demands in her life, or one suffering from depression. She is 'not-good-enough' because she cannot attend to his needs, whereas the 'too-good' mother is often highly anxious about the welfare of her child and cannot tolerate *his* distress. She is 'too-good' in the sense that she will attend too quickly to her infant; she reacts, rather than responds to his pain, getting caught up in it, because she is not grounded herself. As this infant grows into a child he may find it difficult to tolerate discomfort, or to wait for gratification.

Jacobs (1986) links not-good-enough mothering and too-good mothering directly with those who use alcohol and drugs:

> "In reaction or response to mothering which is either neglectful or over-indulgent, and by this we mean not feeding and physical comfort alone, an infant can adopt different defensive ways of coping. These are not specifically linked to neglect or indulgence but can equally apply to both. A child may become clinging or withdrawn. Both defences can be seen at work in those who cling to drugs, alcohol or food." (p35)

The good-enough mother, on the other hand, would be able to hear their child's distress, stay with it and so have psychological contact with him. It is this contact that allows her to really empathise, understand and attune to her infant. As she is not overwhelmed by the infant's affect, she is able to interact with the infant in a calm and reassuring manner. This is a reflection of how she is feeling. While she is attending to his needs her actions will be accompanied by narrative - "Oh dear, you are upset…Don't worry, Mummy's here now" and so on.

In this way the mother establishes a connection for the infant between his physical sensations, his communicating them and his mother attending to his needs and his needs being met. This process enables the infant to make a link between his emotional distress and his physical sensations. Consequently these sensations become valued and can be used by the infant. Life therefore becomes predictable and structured and follows a set narrative for this infant; he feels pain, he communicates this and his needs are met as his care-giver soothes him.

When individuals first engage with our service they are usually in a highly anxious, and/or depressed state. As practitioners, we have an opportunity at this point to begin to provide them with a reparative relationship: to repair the experience that they missed out on in childhood, that is, being looked after and cherished by a good-enough other. In order to be 'good-enough' as practitioners, we need to be reliable and predictable both in what we say and in what we do. Gray comments:

> "I want to stress its importance in the present, in the here-and-now relationship between therapist and client, where it is essential for there to be congruence between the therapist's words and actions." (p7)

Boundaries around time, emotional and physical contact, even the predictability of the room and its furnishings need to be held in place wherever possible.

By allowing individuals to talk about their distress and have someone else make sense of it, they have the experience of their emotions being managed and becoming manageable. This holding experience can also be provided by groups.

> Martin
>
> One day Martin turned up in the group in a highly agitated state. He wriggled and fidgeted in his seat while the other members checked in. When his turn came he was ready to explode. He told us about his frustration towards his wife's employer, who had promised to pay some due wages and had failed to send them. Martin's partner had spoken to them on the phone and had started to cry with frustration and feelings of powerlessness. Martin became overwhelmed by his partner's distress. He told us how he was going to visit the shop with some friends and make a fuss and if they did not give him the money owed, how he would take a bike and sell it himself elsewhere to make up for the missing wages.
>
> The group validated his feelings, told of similar experiences, looked at the consequences of his proposed actions and made alternative suggestions. By the time Martin left the group, he had calmed down and his subsequent behaviour reflected his considered response, rather than his immediate reaction. He had been contained by the group.

At the beginning of the group Martin felt upset but after talking about his concern with the other group members he felt better. This containing experience, if repeated frequently, can often lower general anxiety. The containing process can be highlighted and reinforced by explicitly identifying the different emotional states that were experienced before and after talking things through. Overwhelming, uncontained emotions are often experienced as if they will last for ever so it is useful to make the experience of the transitory nature of emotions more concrete by emphasizing it verbally.

When people are calm enough to take in information, later on in recovery, they can also be given information on how containment works. The experience of containment together with the intellectual understanding can then be processed and internalised so that it can be used in every-day life. Recently, Martin's wife lost a much waited-for baby and he was able to cope with this highly traumatic event without drinking.

An infant who does not have his needs met will adapt creatively to the circumstances and the environment in which he finds himself. This will have a positive reward for the child in the short-term, but the long-term effects might be negative. For example, the infant whose mother is unable to respond to either his physical or emotional needs might learn that it is useless to cry and might find ways to self-soothe, for example sucking his thumb or the sheet. While this might help him to have an experience of being comforted in the short-term, he might grow up expecting his needs not to be met later in life.

When a care-giver is out of tune with what her child needs, the child is confused by the dissonance between what is offered and what is needed. When a child falls over and cuts his leg, if he is offered chocolate instead of comfort, the child can make sense of it in two ways, either he is confused about his capacity to know what he wants, or he can view the mother as confused. The latter conclusion would be a frightening thought for any child at a stage when their survival relies on the competence of this person, so the former is more likely to be internalized. Individuals who have lived with this confusion in early life find it difficult to make even simple decisions, as past experience has taught them that they cannot rely on their own sense of what is needed. In this way the sense of self is lost. They might gradually lose some of their awareness of bodily sensations as they have little or no useful meaning and serve only to heighten their distress. Again their sense of self is diminished.

Not only are these individuals likely to ignore physical sensations because of having a mother who cannot be emotionally present, but also the mother who cannot engage emotionally with her infant hinders the joining up of neural pathways in the brain. Research from neuroscience has shown that the brain develops in, and relies on, the context of a relationship (Schore, 2001). Gerhardt (2004) comments:

> "What needs to be written in neon lights lit up against a night sky is that the orbitofrontal cortex, which is so much about being human, develops almost entirely post-natally." (p37)

The quality of the care-giving we receive affects our capacity to learn and to relate to others. Learning and change throughout life involves letting go of certainty to allow the possibility of new thinking and experiences. Sacret (1999) states that:

> "(A) very problematic consequence of inadequate containment is when any change is felt by the patient to be a step on an inevitable descent into chaos and the terrors of fragmentation. There has to be some sense of psychic continuity for there to be the possibility of change. Otherwise it will be experienced as "catastrophic". (p62)

Regular containment needs to be experienced by some people before change is possible even to consider. A coherent narrative is containing in itself. If a care-giver attends to her/his infant in a series of routines supported by a verbal narrative, the infant is able to predict what will happen next and has a sense of cause and effect. For example, bath-time followed by a warm drink and a story means it is time to sleep. Conversely when life is not held together in this way, it can be experienced as disjointed, random and chaotic. The link between cause and effect is not made. These individuals often have trouble knowing where the boundary is between themselves and others, and can easily become enmeshed. In this case, they find it difficult to distinguish between their own and another's feelings, experiences and needs. If we have a weak sense of self, of our wants and our needs, it is easy to go along with the suggestions of others and fit in with their needs.

Kevin

> Kevin came to therapy because the amount he was drinking had started to affect his capacity to do his job and he was finding it increasingly difficult to hide this from his work colleagues and pupils. Enduring a high level of anxiety he felt that he lived on the edge of a precipice, that he was in constant danger and that he might plunge over the edge at any moment.

> Kevin's narrative included the description of a mother who had had post-natal depression both after his own birth and that of his younger sister. He recounted how his mother told him not to make a fuss if he ever fell over or felt unwell. He described his adolescent years as "terrifying". He often had nightmares and was told not to "cry wolf". As time passed he became unsure how to calibrate his distress, not knowing whether

Addiction - This being human

his own or his mother's sense of reality was correct or whether the truth lay somewhere between the two.

Kevin learnt not to ask for his needs to be met, as he learnt it was unlikely that his mother would be able to provide support. A recurring theme in adult life was that when he talked about his ills, he was rarely heard or made an impact on his audience. When he left home to go to university he started to drink more heavily. Kevin learnt to drink whenever he felt emotionally vulnerable in order to dull the pain.

Kevin's early experience did not include someone who was able to stay calm and hold him physically or emotionally. He had little sense of who he was. Although Kevin was able to communicate his needs, his mother was unable to respond due to her own internal depression and distress.

Michelle

Michelle grew up in a family with a "naughty" sister. The sister was always in trouble at school, became pregnant as a young teenager and then moved in with an older man. Michelle's perception of these events was that they caused his mother overwhelming amounts of distress.

Michelle experienced her mother as "fragile" and unable to cope with any more trouble. She learnt to be "good" as she felt that there was already enough strain on the family. In order to avoid conflict within the family she learnt to "go with the flow" even if it was against her self-interest.

Later in life she felt more and more resentful of

> people taking advantage of her, as she fitted in with everyone else's plans and never said "No!" However, as she had no outlet for what she perceived to be her negative emotions, she learnt through her social drinking habits that occasionally an intoxicated state would allow her to vent her anger. It got acted out by doing "naughty" things such as drinking heavily or gambling. When she recovered from her bouts of drinking the predominant emotion was no longer anger, but shame and guilt.

In Michelle's case, she felt unable to let her mother know when she was emotionally upset and why, so her mother was not given the opportunity to act as a container.

If we have had the experience of a parent who can soothe us, we learn to self-soothe. On the other hand, if we have not, we are left feeling overwhelmed by our emotions. Not having had the experience of having our emotions contained, we have no past experience of coping to draw on later in life. As thinking in psychotherapy develops around the concept of containment, it is more generally acknowledged that the inability of the mother to contain the child is traumatising in itself:

> "(F)ailures in the psychic environment of the child, often linked with inadequate containment or other failures…can have a traumatising effect." (Sacret, p73)

A large proportion of individuals who seek help with substance misuse have not only had a primary care-giver who was unable to contain their emotions, but they have sometimes also had a primary care-giver who, due to their own personal histories, has been highly punitive or cruel. Mark was made to stand on a certain step on the stairs for hours and was hit when he moved.

Addiction - This being human

Darren was locked into a dark attic room without a candle for large stretches of time. Bruce had hot tea straight from a teapot poured down his throat. Richard was tied to a chair and force fed. Carol was put into boiling hot baths. The stories go on. Part of how we know who we are is a consequence of how we are treated; these individuals may come to see themselves as worthy of nothing better. The consequent acts of self-harm by people who have suffered this kind of cruelty can be seen as a result of them acting out the internalised voices of their cruel care-givers.

Britton (1992) has suggested that:

> "(I)f this relationship between mother and the infant goes badly wrong, instead of a helpful superego, an 'ego-destructive superego' develops…when containment goes wrong in some people, it produces a part of themselves opposed to themselves." (p107)

The failure in this initial relationship has other implications. Perry et al. (1995) found that those of us who do not have the capacity to self-soothe may be over-sensitive to and stimulated by perceived potential threats. These individuals are, then, more likely to feel fear in every-day situations.

The theories of 'containment' and the 'good-enough mother' can help us appreciate that personalities are not set in stone and can change; the capacity to internalise a reparative, kind and encouraging care-giver continues throughout life. Neural pathways can be linked up, given an appropriate future facilitating relationship. One of our main functions when working with individuals that seek help with substance misuse must be to provide containment, in groups and in one-to-one relationships so that participants can feel safe, internalise a nurturing voice, gain a stronger sense of who they are and ultimately learn to self-soothe.

Additionally, if we bear these theories in mind, we are more able to empathise and be compassionate with individuals that use substances to deal with their emotions. We are likewise far less likely to demand, or expect, behaviours that they cannot maintain until they have had the repeated experience of being contained by a group or an individual.

Further reading:

BATEMAN A. & HOLMES J. (1995) *Introduction to Psychoanalysis.* London: Routledge.

WINNICOTT D.W. (1960) 'The Theory of the Parent-Infant Relationship.' In *The Maturational Processes and the Facilitating Environment.* London: Hogarth, 1965.

4

OUR STATE OF MIND

> Men often become what they believe themselves to
> be. If I believe I cannot do something, it makes me
> incapable of doing it. But when I believe I can, then
> I acquire the ability to do it even if I didn't have it in
> the beginning.
> ~Mahatma Gandi

So that we can engage with individuals seeking help at the point where they are psychologically, and recognise when they are living with their fear system in operation, it is useful to look at the work of Melanie Klein (1946), Karpman (1968) and Berne (1970).

> Klein, through her work with infants, identified two developmental positions from which we relate to our primary care-giver. She called them 1) the paranoid-schizoid position, and 2) the depressive position. She found evidence to suggest that in the first six months of our lives we cannot hold on to the idea of a mother that consists of 'bad' and 'good' parts. As infants, to experience ourselves as dependent on someone who is seen, at times, as bad, feels too dangerous and can feel

life threatening. Infants defend against this anxiety of trying to hold good and bad together by 'splitting'. They literally split the mother into two different parts and experience her as two different people: the 'good' mother when she is being comforting and nurturing and the 'bad' mother when she is absent, or is present but not being nurturing.

Klein believed that as infants we have unconscious fantasies that the 'bad' mother is withholding nourishment and keeping it all for herself. This makes sense if we think of the contrast between our pre-natal experiences in the womb where we were warm, fed, kept at a constant temperature and where life was on the whole predictable, and how this changes at birth. This fantasised competition with the mother for resources, stirs up anxiety. Klein called this anxiety 'persecutory anxiety' because at times the infant can feel persecuted by the bad mother.

How we deal with this persecutory anxiety, Klein suggests, is by idealising the 'good' mother and by denying the extent of the 'bad' mother's power by attacking her with psychic fantasies. The infant relates to the mother according to his perception of which mother is present and so his response is then split; between hate and love. We can easily recognise the wicked step-mother and the fairy god-mother archetypes because of this early experience.

Klein further states that the depressive position develops as a natural progression from the paranoid-schizoid position as we are able to focus our vision, and come to recognise the mother as the same person. We gradually accept that both bad and good elements can exist in the same person. With this acceptance of the integrated mother come feelings of guilt around the previous unconscious desire to harm the bad mother. At this stage, we feel the need to repair and make up

Addiction - This being human

for our destructive fantasies. Klein explains that we all move between these two positions throughout life. We regress to the paranoid-schizoid position in times of stress. In a conflict situation it is easy to see the other person as holding all the bad because we have regressed to a place where we feel threatened. For example, if we are involved in an acrimonious divorce it is difficult at the time to remember, and hold on to, the good characteristics of our ex-partner.

Many people who go on to use substances are living in circumstances that induce high levels of stress – inadequate housing, overcrowding, unemployment, unbalanced diets and so on. There are also often high levels of conflict between family members. It is easy to understand then how these individuals might often experience high stress and anxiety, and how their earliest defences of denial and splitting might be triggered and prove useful.

As we saw earlier, an inability to self-soothe is linked to our increased perception of threat. This means that individuals who have not had 'good-enough' mothering are more likely to stay in, or regress to, Klein's paranoid-schizoid position and for their fight- flight response to be more often naturally engaged. This category includes many individuals who use substances to cope with their emotional life. They will spend more of their time in Klein's paranoid-schizoid position, than those of us under less stress. The paranoia that they experience comes from their fear system and is a natural and necessary element of the fear process – in dangerous situations it helps to keep them safe.

The fight-flight response is designed to help us get out of immediate danger and therefore effective if short lived but if we live in a state of stress our bodies produce adrenaline continuously. This affects us both physically and psychologically.

What helps in a threatening situation includes tunnel-vision as we need to stay focused on the threat, becoming critical so that we can identify weak spots, reacting rather than responding as we may not have time to think and losing empathy so we can use aggressive behaviour (Gilbert, 2001). If our stress system operates most of the time these behaviours become habitual and do not serve us.

One of the defences against fear, as we have seen from Klein's work, is to deny that the perceived threat exists. When denial is used repeatedly, it can become entrenched. As professionals, we commonly see denial used in terms of the amount of substance that any individual is using and the effect that this has on their day-to-day functioning. Denial often exists around other issues too.

> Jill
>
> When Jill came to us, her main aim was to discover why she drank. She could understand that less fortunate people drank to "drown their sorrows", but was mystified by her own habit. She considered her own self-esteem was high and suggested she had enjoyed a happy childhood.
>
> During the course of therapy, it emerged that she had a disabled brother who was only several months older. She came to realise how this had affected her relationship with her parents and her brother. His neediness meant that her needs were put on hold, while his had been attended to promptly. Eventually she was able to voice the resentments she held on to about this "unfairness". Later she also disclosed that she had witnessed the death of her first love under circumstances she was powerless to address. She

Addiction - This being human

> used denial to play down the scale of her distress. Consequently the grieving process was interrupted and again her emotional needs were put on hold.
>
> Later denial no longer served her as she could hide from herself how much she was drinking. When Jill became sober, if she lapsed, she could go into denial about how far she had come on her recovery journey.

We can see how the defence of denial, which had helped Jill resist the impact of powerful emotional feelings as a child, became disabling. In adulthood denial made her perceptions unrealistic and affected her ability to either process early painful childhood experiences or to grieve for her lost partner. Ultimately, in therapy she also came to a more realistic view of her childhood experiences and the state of her self-esteem.

The other defence identified with the paranoid-schizoid position by Klein was splitting. When we are in the depressive position we can hold onto the idea that all circumstances, or people, have the potential to be threatening, when they are not necessarily threatening. However, if we are already feeling paranoid and experiencing circumstances, and/or people, to be actually threatening, it would follow that our daily life might appear too dangerous unless we split situations and relationships into 'good' and 'bad'. When leaving our premises people often make comments like "I feel safe and good about myself in here, but when I leave the building it's a different story. Life is so scary *out there*."

Splitting also manifests itself in what has been called 'all-or-nothing' thinking. For example, if Jill had a lapse, she might not only lose sight of her achievements, but also claim that she is always useless. She struggles to maintain a more realistic and balanced view that sometimes she does not achieve her goals and sometimes she does.

When individuals who use splitting enter treatment, they often experience themselves, for much of the time, as all 'bad', and their primary care-giver as all 'good'. As they come to see that we all have human qualities - we all have strengths and weaknesses, they start to develop greater compassion for themselves and begin to re-evaluate the unconscious messages they internalised about themselves according to how they were treated by their care-givers. For example, if you feel you have not been loved, you unconsciously take in the message that you are unlovable. Once individuals start to appreciate that their care-giver might have been talking and acting out of their own emotional pain; they come to see that their parents' actions and criticisms had little to do with their own 'badness'.

It is useful to see these behaviours of denial and splitting as prompted by high levels of anxiety, rather than to think of them as either deliberate acts of withholding information or just plain lying. We can identify these two positions described by Klein in a concept noted by Karpman (1968) and expanded by Eric Berne (1970): the Drama Triangle. Berne describes a dynamic that is common in unhealthy relationships and one which he particularly links to substance abuse. This kind of dynamic is what Berne calls a "game". He comments that it is as if an unconscious play is being performed where the actors are so well rehearsed they can take on all the different roles. Each role is dependent on the other and all are facilitated by denial and splitting. For example, the victim splits off their capacity to achieve and to be assertive. Someone in a victim frame of mind will unconsciously draw people into 'rescue' them or to 'persecute' them which confirms their role as someone who cannot be responsible for, or fend for, themselves and who is a victim.

Anne and Ruby

Anne referred herself to our project when she was drinking a bottle of sherry a day. She was 64 and had recently moved into the city, partly to help out her son, who had been commuting from many miles away. She was very lonely, depressed and had a very high level of anxiety. She had previously been diagnosed with manic-depression, but was not taking her medication. Anne had a few loose teeth and had not eaten solid food for several weeks, because she was scared of losing them. She was on a liquid diet and complained constantly about finding food boring and about her lack of motivation to cook for herself.

The first day in the group, Anne shared her desperation by asking other members of the group what they ate. People offered their suggestions, but they were all rejected with comments like "Oh…do you like that …I find that too boring", or "Oh…I don't have the motivation to cook, I'm on my own dear". These comments were usually made with a look of disgust on her face. Ruby, one of the group members, became agitated by Anne's apparent distress. The next day Ruby brought in a meal she had cooked for Anne at home.

Here we can see that Ruby has taken on the rescuer's role. She found it difficult to stay with Anne's distress and so *she* found a solution for it. In this way, she unconsciously confirmed Anne in the role of victim, as someone who could not cook for herself. Anne did not have to take responsibility for managing her own distress if she could rely on another. Anne was able to shop and cook for herself, but she chose not to. Anne later admitted that she had given the meal to her son.

Those who 'rescue' others do so for their own sake. They feel distress at the other's discomfort, project their *own* distress onto the other and then try to alleviate it so that they can regain their *own* equilibrium. We might note the similarity between this rescuing behaviour and the too-good mother's behaviour.

We can see parallels too between the victim role and Klein's paranoid-schizoid position; in both places the individual feels persecutory anxiety. There are also similar parallels between the rescuer and Klein's depressive position; where individuals need to repair or make something better for the other person. These two different theories, taken from different orientations, do seem to support each other.

It is not unusual for people caught in this dynamic to slip from one of the roles on the Drama Triangle to another: they might alternate between the victim, the persecutor and the rescuer. In the same way, Klein notes we move between her two positions throughout life. We can appreciate how, if Ruby had felt the need to cook for Anne constantly, Ruby might eventually have felt resentful and might have shown her anger in some way, thereby becoming the persecutor. Any aggression shown to Anne would have confirmed her in the victim role in the same way that cooking a meal for her did. In this case, this was not acted out because shortly after this incident, Ruby left the group and returned to work.

In dysfunctional families where there is actual physical, emotional or sexual abuse or neglect, this drama is acted out again and again *for real*. There is a real victim and a real

Addiction - This being human

persecutor and these roles become so well-rehearsed that they continue even if the abuse stops, or the individuals concerned leave that particular family or group. These roles can be carried over into other relationships and can be carried from generation to generation. It is experienced and accepted as a 'normal' way to be in a relationship with another. It is normal, after all, for those who know nothing else.

Neil and Kate

In Neil's childhood, he had suffered a lot of verbal and physical abuse from a father who was often drunk. When the father returned from the pub Neil and his siblings would disappear into their bedroom. This time of day was very unpredictable. Sometimes it would pass off without incident, but on other occasions the mother or Neil would be cornered and they would be beaten. If the mother tried to comfort Neil afterwards, the father would lash into her.

At the time Neil came for help, he was in a similar abusive relationship. He lived with his partner, Kate. She demanded an unreasonable rent even at times when he was out of work. They slept in separate beds and she showed him no affection. She opened his post and was unhappy if he talked to another woman. Eventually she got a menial job in the factory where he worked so that she could 'keep an eye on him.

Sharing a home with this partner re-created Neil's experience of living in fear. Kate came to represent his violent father and so his emotional response to her was the same as it had been to his father. Neil would drink to deal with his anxiety. On one occasion Neil was looking forward to a reunion with some old friends. Partners were not invited. In a moment of rage about the thought of Neil going without her, Kate shredded his uniform. This made it impossible for Neil to attend, not only because of his lack of correct dress but also because faced with rage displayed in this way, Neil became overwhelmed by the feelings of terror associated with his father's beatings and he felt impotent to attend the reunion.

The roles of persecutor and rescuer can be played out by the same person, or by several people within a single family. When Kate felt threatened by Neil leaving, she would temporarily become a charming, caring rescuer. At other times she would attack him verbally and physically. In Neil's birth family, the role of victim and rescuer were alternately played by Neil and his mother, depending on who the father chose to attack. On rare occasions, when resentment reached a peak, Neil would snap and lash out at Kate such that she would become the victim.

A relationship with an addictive substance can mirror the relationships acted out in the Drama Triangle, only here the individual using the substance creates, with the help of the substance, all the roles in relation to himself. For example, if a large bill arrives in the post it can be experienced in a persecutory way by the receiver. Unable to cope with the feelings that this brings up, an individual who finds anxiety difficult to cope with will reach for a drink. The drink becomes the rescuer. Once the drinker reaches the point where he is no longer in control of how much he drinks, the alcohol itself can be experienced as persecutory. If we have been the victim in our birth families, it is easy to see how using a substance would feel familiar and safe and why we might choose that form of self-harming behaviour over another.

Addiction - This being human

It is essential to be aware of this potential dynamic when working in this field, otherwise it is easy to be pulled or pushed into the drama. If we are working in the caring professions it is likely that we took on the role of the rescuer in our birth families. We are often drawn to work in situations where our roles feel familiar and with those with whom we can identify. So it is easy for our own needs to be projected onto individuals who come for help. It is as if we see our own needs in them. In these circumstances, it is easy for us to be drawn into the rescuing role and gain satisfaction from watching the other feel 'better', rather than attending to our own distress. It may be that this feeling 'better' is a step backwards, rather than forwards, for the very person that we intended to help. For example, if we comfort someone at the wrong moment, we may halt what might otherwise have been a cathartic process.

Equally it is possible to be pulled into the role of persecutor as we become frustrated by another's negative perception of their situation. We might snap at them, for example. If we can remember that narrative is a reflection of lived experience and listen in an empathic and compassionate way to individuals who are exhibiting the behaviour of the Drama Triangle roles, they will be unable to stay in that frame of mind. By refusing to play the game, we leave them without a role and the opportunity to do something different about their situation.

It is highly likely that people working in the caring professions generally, and the addiction field particularly, will have played a part in the Drama Triangle at some stage in their birth family. If we can understand, recognise and acknowledge this dynamic then we are more able to notice when we are pulled into it. For example, we are more likely to notice when we are putting more and more effort into helping one particular individual.

Sarah and Jeff

Sarah noticed she was putting in more and more effort with one of her clients, Jeff. She also found that she was starting to side with him whenever he recounted an incident between him and his partner.

We explored this together in supervision and she came to see how Jeff reminded her of her own father. Jeff was in the army, as Sarah's own father had been. He spoke in a gentle voice and rarely expressed his anger. Jeff seemed to be trapped in a similar bullying relationship to the one that Sarah had witnessed between her own father and mother.

Sarah quickly came to see how she had lost her perspective and objectivity as her feelings towards her own mother resurfaced in reference to Jeff's partner. Sarah had played the rescuer role towards her father and was now replaying this role in her relationship with Jeff. Once Sarah became conscious of this recreated role, she could work with Jeff in a more productive way, helping him to see the part he was playing in the relationship with his partner.

Our unconscious is very powerful. It is both understandable and likely that we will start to rescue an individual if we can identify with them or if they remind us of the original figure that we rescued. To be more conscious of when we are rescuing, it is useful to be aware of when our help has been asked for, as opposed to when we are acting primarily to lower our own level of frustration or anxiety. Another useful question to ask ourselves is whether the task we are doing is one that the individual could have done for himself, but is choosing not to.

If we are unaware of this dynamic, or lacking in self-awareness, the relationship, which was intended to be healing, might instead repeat the abuse and this would result in the further disempowerment, rather than the personal growth, of the individual who has come for help.

Hawkins and Shohet (2000) make the point that:

> "(I)t is essential for all those in the helping professions to reflect honestly on the complex mixture of motives that have led them to their current profession and role. For as Guggenbuhl-Craig (1971) writes: 'no one can act out of exclusively pure motives. The greater the contamination by dark motives, the more the case worker clings to his alleged objectivity." (p9)

As our unconscious self is too powerful for us to be consistently objective about our emotional reactions, it is essential for us as professionals to acknowledge the need to monitor our own therapeutic interactions with the help of appropriate supervision.

Further reading:

BATEMAN A. & HOLMES J. (1995) *Introduction to Psychoanalysis.* London: Routledge.

BERNE E (1970) *The Games People Play.* London: Penguin Books

GILBERT P. (2001) Evolutionary approaches to psychopathology: the role of natural defences. In *Australian and New Zealand Journal of Psychiatry. 35: pp17-27.*

KARPMAN S. (1968) Fairy Tales and Script Drama Analysis. In *Transactional Analysis Bulletin, vol. 7, no. 26, pp. 39-43.*

KLEIN M. (1946) Some notes on Schizoid Mechanisms. In *Envy and Gratitude and Other Works 1946-1963.* London: Vintage 1997.

5

OUR BODY STORY-LINES AND MEMORY

> You do not have to be good.
> You do not have to walk on your knees
> for a hundred miles through the desert repenting.
> You only have to let the soft animal of your body
> love what it loves.
> ~Mary Oliver

Just as we have psychological defences, like denial or rationalisation, our body also has physical defences. Our emotions can become frozen in our breath and/or muscles, which affect our body posture.

Totten and Edmondson (1988) describe how the early experience of the infant becomes held in the breath:

> "Imagine a baby who cries out as her natural way of expressing her need – hunger, cold, desire for company – and no-one comes. It will take a long time for this to sink in: she will cry and cry again, but eventually she will stop. She suppresses her crying by holding her breath – which holds back her grief and anger, not

> identified consciously as feelings, but implicit in the whole state of her body. Now imagine another baby who is picked up and manipulated by cold hands: not so much physically cold, but emotionally cold, uncaring. Babies feel these things, and there will be a reaction of shock, a gasp, like the gasp if we step into cold water. If this experience is repeated often enough, then that gasp, that held breath, will become built into the baby's body nature." (p9)

In this way our personal histories become mirrored in our breathing. Similarly, as we repeatedly tense the same muscles to protect ourselves, the muscles become hardened. This is a defence, which affects the way we hold our body and can keep the experiencing of sensation at a distance. Reich (1947) describes the effect of successively holding ourselves together during traumatic events as body armouring.

> Jason
>
> Jason was brought up in a violent, unpredictable household. His father had been unemployed and spent a lot of the time drinking and was frequently violent towards his mother or one of the children, including Jason after drinking excessively. The family could only relax when he was sleeping it off on the sofa or floor.
>
> When Jason first joined the Swan Project, it was as if his natural breathing pattern had been arrested. His chest was permanently puffed out and his chest cavity was never relaxed. It looked as if the many gasps Jason had taken in childhood out of fear were now permanently stuck his shoulders were tight and his fists were often clenched.

Jason's defiant stance was a defence against fear. The use of intentional touch in the form of massage, which brings attention to our skin boundary can help us feel 'together', contained and bring back to life the parts of the body that have been numbed in a traumatic situation, or a chain of less traumatic events. By doing gentle breathing exercises each day and having weekly massage, Jason was gradually able to release and relax his breathing and muscles. His fists became unclenched and with it his experience of daily life became less fearful. As his fear dropped, his state of mind, his physiology and his behaviours changed. He told us that he was able to sit in a public space without his back to the wall as he no longer felt constantly under threat. As his fear subsided, he had the psychological space to reflect and make decisions, rather than just react to threatening stimuli.

Once we consciously relax our muscles, or in more dramatic circumstances, we start to manipulate our body back into its original state, the emotions that have been frozen can start to move through the body. I had a profound experience of this myself.

> After rising too quickly from my seat, my leg gave way under the weight of my body and I started to limp. A few days later, I went to see a chiropractor who looked at my body and asked me whether I had ever had an accident with my jaw, as it was out of balance. I remembered my jaw becoming unhooked when I had been nearing the end of my secondary education. He told me that this accident had affected the way I carried myself. My whole body was out of alignment, including my hips and this was why my leg had buckled. Over the course of a few weeks he gradually manipulated my jaw back to its original symmetrical position.

Over these weeks, I started to feel quite paranoid and could not understand why. Luckily, I told the chiropractor about it. He asked me if I had felt paranoia at the time when I had injured my jaw. Incredibly, to me at the time, I realised I had.

I remembered the incident with my jaw very well because it had been such a significant event. When I was 15, I was given the main speaking part in the school play. My teachers praised my acting and I felt good about myself. The evening before the first night, I yawned too wide and my jaw had become unhooked. This meant that I was unable to take the part in the play, as the injury to my jaw affected my ability to open my mouth widely and therefore my capacity to speak loudly.

My initial paranoia, at the time of the injury, had been triggered by my fear of being verbally attacked by my adoptive mother. I had often felt verbally and emotionally attacked by her, especially on those occasions when I excelled at something. As I considered my current paranoia with this incident in mind, I realised that my fifteen year old body/mind had unhooked my jaw as a defence: if I couldn't be the star of the play, I would not be verbally attacked by my mother.

The paranoia which would have passed through my body had I been able to stay with the experience, had frozen inside my body instead. As my body was manipulated back into balance, the frozen emotion could now be experienced and pass through me. My body memory of how it had felt the last time it had been in that position, evoked the emotion to do with that part of my history, in the same way that a remembered smell, or a piece of music can.

The word emotion comes from the Latin - '*e*' which means 'out' and '*movere*' which means 'to move'. Emotions naturally move through the body – they perform the function of a messenger. It is our physical or psychological defence against the pain that results in them becoming permanent and stuck. If we are able to sit with and bear our emotions they will pass in a wave, rising and then falling in intensity. Kepner explains:

> "The feeling of sadness becomes the act of crying when we allow the sensations to develop naturally into the contractions of the breathing musculature, vocal sobs and facial expressions of grief. The feeling of longing, when allowed to develop into movement, includes reaching out physically for the loved one. It is only through full movement that feeling has full meaning. Only by moving can we connect the need the feeling manifests to the environment where needs can be completed." (p16)

In the same way that my chiropractor's manipulations worked, massage can release frozen emotions. As muscles that have become hard from constant tensing as a defence are relaxed and slowly return to their looser form, emotions that have been stuck are able to move and pass through the body.

To manage, contain and process our emotions, we need to be in touch with our sensations and emotions at a subtle level – at a point where they are not already overwhelming. Bernhardt (1995) comments:

> "Body awareness provides the bridge between cognition and emotion, and is the platform from

> which various impulses and associations can be integrated and metabolised." (p54)

Bodywork, for example, focusing, breathing exercises, massage, reiki and other therapies that work on the skin boundary can help to reconnect us with our body sensations. Once we can be in touch with subtle emotions and make the link between the bodily sensation and its cause, we are more easily able to bear the emotion, think about it and so process it, allowing the emotion to flow through us. As Rogers (1961) puts it:

> "A feeling which has previously been 'stuck', has been inhibited in its process quality, is experienced with immediacy now. A feeling flows to its full result." (p145)

When this happens we gain the sense that emotions are momentary, temporary feelings. As we become more contained and more in touch with our bodies, we can learn to sit with the wave of emotions and gain a sense of our emotional self.

We can gradually re-develop our body awareness by paying attention to it in a systematic way. For example, we might notice the difference in temperature between the soles and the top of our feet, how our socks feel - whether they are tight, soft or worn in parts and so on, as we move our attention up towards our head. As we become more aware of the body's intelligent feedback, we can start to make sense of it. We might notice our arm aches and remember that we spent long hours on the computer yesterday, or feel angry and link it to our agreement to do a favour for a friend which we now regret. Once we have made these associations, we can then choose not to use the computer so much, or to retract the offer of help. When we can think about what is happening in our body then we can process and integrate the experience and put it to rest. It no longer disturbs our equilibrium. As we become more familiar with this process and consequently experience emotions as more contained, our self-harming behaviours become reduced to a more socially acceptable and manageable level, or even become redundant.

Often at the beginning of counselling, an individual has trouble making sense of their feelings, because there is a time lag between the trigger and the feeling. Imagine for example, that an upsetting remark is made by a colleague. If the emotional upset response happens immediately, we can make the connection with the incident with our colleague, but if we finish our work, go home on the bus and the emotional impact catches up with us as we are having supper, it is difficult to make the link with what has upset us. If the individual is supported to explore the link between the emotional distress and its cause, and is helped to become more in touch with her emotions at a subtle level, the experience of the body/mind and what is happening at the time gradually become closer. When this happens it becomes possible to think about emotional experiences and to process them more immediately. Eventually the individual feels the emotions at the same time as an upsetting comment is made, and can address the issue promptly. In this way, life is no longer experienced as random and chaotic.

By focusing on our bodies and noticing the location and the quality of our energy, our physical sensations and our feelings, we can get in touch with what Gendlin (1996) calls our 'felt sense'. A felt sense is a kind of bodily awareness. It is not a mental experience but a physical one. Gendlin describes it as:

> "An internal aura that encompasses everything you feel and know about a given subject at a given time – encompasses it and communicates it to you all at once

rather than detail after detail. Think of it as a taste, if you like, or a great musical chord that makes you feel a powerful impact, a big round unclear feeling. A felt sense doesn't come to you in the form of thoughts or other simple units, but as a single (though often puzzling and very complex) bodily feeling." (p32-33).

Our felt sense helps us to understand who we are in that moment, how we are feeling and what is called for to meet our needs.

Helena

Helena's father had left the family when she was small. She had a long history of using alcohol to help her cope with distress. As she worked at becoming more aware of her bodily sensations her behaviour changed. Three months into treatment, it was Helena's birthday. Helena had always found birthdays difficult as they brought up memories of her sitting with a packed suitcase, waiting for her father to arrive to pick her up. He frequently failed to turn up which left Helena feeling pain for which she had no words. In the course of her therapy she came to understand why she felt pain and the name of the emotions that she felt; rejection and abandonment.

Accordingly, she anticipated that this birthday was going to be a potential trigger for a lapse as she re-experienced the abandonment. On the actual day she and her partner had a row and went their separate ways for the rest of the day. She did feel abandoned by her partner in the moment but because the situation had been anticipated and talked through with her counsellor, she did not pick up a drink. Although the thought of a drink flashed through Helena's mind, her logic and her body told her it would not help and she resisted.

Helena responded differently to the feelings of abandonment on this occasion from the way she had reacted on previous occasions. Earlier in her recovery, she would have 'needed' a drink as her partner walked off. By contrast, on this occasion she was able to remain sober for several reasons. She had anticipated the situation and was conscious of what was happening emotionally for her. She recognised the overwhelming feelings as those of abandonment and could link them to the past. She was supported by her knowledge that alcohol would not help the situation. By getting in touch with her felt sense, she intuitively knew that alcohol was not what she wanted, or needed. She was able to respond to the situation rather than just react because she was able to stay grounded and was not overwhelmed by her emotions. She contained her emotions herself.

The next day after making up, they went out for a meal together. Helena chose to order a glass of wine with the meal. She went on to order a second, but as she drank it, she recoiled from it and realised that she did not want it and so she left it on the table. On this occasion Helena had chosen to drink socially. She was not drinking to cope with emotional difficulties. It was her body - the effect on her tongue and her head - that told her not to carry on drinking and her logical thinking confirmed that a second glass would only lead to more. Again Helena's body sense and her mind were congruent: the body/mind split was not operating. However, part of the reason why she could access her felt sense and control her alcohol intake on this occasion was because she was not using the alcohol to cope. Also she was grounded and her fear system was not operating so she could respond rather than react. When our fight-flight response is operating, we are designed to react, rather than to respond, in order for us to get out of a dangerous situation as quickly as possible. Our logic is put on hold. When our fight-flight response is active it is more likely that we will fall back on habitual behaviour.

The physical contact provided by massage has the capacity to bring the individual's awareness to his body so that he has more of a sense of his skin boundary. It allows him to feel grounded and gradually build up his sense of self. "This is me." "This is where I start and this is where I end." If we have a strong sense of self, we can take responsibility for our actions more readily, we project fewer unwanted emotions on to others; we come to realise our own wants, rather than going along with the flow. We are more able to get our needs met.

Body memory is also a useful concept when thinking about and working with addictions. Rothschild (2002), in describing body memory states that:

> "There are basically two categories of memory: explicit and implicit. Explicit memory is conscious and requires language. It is comprised of concepts, facts, events, descriptions and thoughts. Implicit memory on the other hand is unconscious. It is made up of emotions, sensations, movements and automatic procedures. The term body memory and somatic memory suggest the implicit." (p105)

To change habits we need to remember that time span memories are held in the body. In the same way that sounds and smells can evoke memories, so can the passing of time. Drawing a scaled time line from birth to the present and plotting losses on the line often reveals a pattern. Most patterns have historical roots. If the relationship with the primary carer ceased after two years through death or ill health, for example, it is as if the body/mind starts to get restless in subsequent relationships around the two year mark. The person can unconsciously anticipate being abandoned after this interval and can leave the relationship or the job before the anticipated abandonment can take place. So in this case, for example, what the individual might notice is that they never stay in relationships or jobs for longer than two years. When we become conscious of patterns of behaviour that helped us once but now no longer serve us we can choose whether we wish to repeat them or take a different path.

David

One of David's saddest memories, captured in a photo, was of himself sitting on his father's knee as a small child. In his father's hand was a bottle of whiskey. David commented that he looked out of place, just perched on the lap somehow, whereas the bottle looked almost as if it was an extension of his father's arm. Whenever David looked at this photo, he felt sad as he recognised the psychological distance between himself and his father.

After drawing his time line, David discovered that he had started drinking heavily when his first son reached seven years old. This was the age at which his own father had left his mother, abandoning him. Unconsciously David had repeated the pattern with his own son by abandoning him at the same age.

When these time memories remain unconscious, they can sabotage an individual's recovery. Cravings can be set off, or intensified by a body memory – our body predicting our course of action. So that if we only drink at weekends, we might find that the thought of drinking rarely intrudes during the working week, but as Friday approaches we start to have bodily cravings. Our bodies hold story-lines as memories that anticipate what will happen next.

Charlotte

Charlotte had made several attempts to stop drinking. Her longest period of abstinence had been six months. When we met Charlotte had been in a rehabilitation centre for four months and was doing well. She did still have cravings, but was able to manage them. However, as she approached six months of abstinence, Charlotte's cravings became unbearable.

She could not understand how after all this time they could suddenly be so strong. As we made the link between her previous period of abstinence and the time she had been sober this time, she was able to make sense of what was happening to her. Her body was predicting that she would start drinking again as she had the last time after a six month period. Once Charlotte understood that this was only going to be a temporary period of intense cravings, she was able to cope. As predicted, once she passed over this six month bookmark, the cravings subsided back to their normal level.

If Charlotte had not known about the impact of body memories, she could have given up at that point, thinking that the intensity of the cravings was random and might stay at that level of intensity or become more intense. Once she became aware of why the cravings had intensified at that particular point in time, she was able to bear them, in the knowledge that they would only last in the short term.

There is another useful way to think about the process of change. This way includes the concepts of unconscious incompetence, conscious incompetence, conscious competence and unconscious competence. After the initial honeymoon period of maintenance when we notice the benefits of not drinking, it can be a struggle to carry on. This is partly because during this stage of change we need to be constantly vigilant so that we do not slip back into old behaviour. Once we realise that eventually we will reach unconscious competence the journey seems easier. For example, while learning to drive our level of concentration is intense until the process becomes habitual. In the same way, not using a substance to self-soothe in time also becomes habitual.

If we are trying to cut back or halt an addictive behaviour, it is useful to change as much in our immediate surroundings as we can– the opposite of the predictability of the counselling room. This will keep us more vigilant. If we change the cupboard we keep the glasses in, put the bottles or cans in a different room, have a pot of strong smelling coffee on the go, pick up our glass with the wrong hand, drink standing up and from a mug and so on, we will find it much easier to change our habit. These, and similar conscious and active choices, prevent us from slipping into old habits which feel as if we are on automatic pilot and not in control. As in all new learning, we need to become consciously competent before we can integrate the process and develop a new habitual way of being.

Physical therapies, like massage, reiki, reflexology and other interventions that work on the skin boundary can also offer vital support to help us to reconnect to our bodily sensations and emotions. Regular sessions can provide, or can reinforce, the experience of being in an undemanding relationship that is safe and nurturing. We experience acceptance just for being who we are, rather than having to perform in any way.

Further reading:

GENDLIN E. (1996) *Focusing Orientated Psychotherapy*. London: The Guildford Press.

KEPNER J.I. (1987) *Body Process – Working with Body in Psychotherapy*. San Francisco: Jossey Bass Publishers

TOTTEN N. & EDMONDSON (1988) *Reichian Growth Work*. Bridport: Prism Press.

TREE STAUNTON (Ed.) (2002) *Body Psychotherapy*. Sussex: Brunner-Routledge.

6

OUR SHAME PROCESS

> "What are you doing there?" he said to the tippler, whom he found settled down in silence before a collection of empty bottles and also a collection of full bottles. "I am drinking," replied the tippler, with a lugubrious air. "Why are you drinking?" demanded the little prince. "So that I may forget," replied the tippler. "Forget what?" inquired the little prince, who already was sorry for him. "Forget that I am ashamed," the tippler confessed, hanging his head. "Ashamed of what?" insisted the little prince, who wanted to help him. "Ashamed of drinking!" The tippler brought his speech to an end, and shut himself up in an impregnable silence.
> ~Antoine De Saint-Exupery

> You are a child of the universe, no less than the trees and the stars; you have a right to be here.
> ~Max Ehrmann

Through my work with individuals who are using substances to cope with their anxiety I have learnt the importance of holding in mind the concept and nature of shame. This powerful emotion can prompt excessive drinking or drug taking. If sobriety is set as a goal and a lapse occurs shame can also prevent help being sought when it is most needed.

As infants and growing children, the way in which we experience our parents' actions and verbal messages will affect our sense of self, our sense of who we are. Kohut (1971) identifies 'mirroring' as one of the mother's crucial functions. When the mother looks at her child with love and adoration, it is as if the baby sees himself in a mirror. The smile tells him he is special and loved and that he is worthy of her attention. Sadly, the opposite is also true.

Negative responses to our childhood behaviour and criticism from authority figures, especially from the primary care-giver, become internalised. This is a necessary part of the way we learn and adapt to the social environment in which we find ourselves. In a healthy situation these negative comments will not be excessive and will be balanced by praise for our achievements. In this way the infant comes to understand that making mistakes is part of being human; they are part and parcel of how we learn. However, when criticism and shaming are excessive, they can have a debilitating effect on the child's development and his sense of self. In these circumstances it is probable that we will perceive ourselves as not 'good enough' and we may fear abandonment. Given that our very survival depends on being acceptable and 'taken in' by our care-giver, this feeling of inadequacy, and the distress it provokes, can become part of how we see our essential being when criticism is a constant theme.

Most of us who have been excessively shamed come in to therapy dreading that this 'bad' part of ourselves will be discovered. As we are not quite sure what it is, other than an uncomfortable felt sense, we feel that we cannot protect ourselves from exposing this imagined part. Totten and Edmondson use the example of unacceptable anger:

> "If this anger is itself suppressed, we end up with a superficial layer of socialised 'niceness' covering up all sorts of hateful and vicious feelings, created out of anger which cannot discharge itself, stewing and stagnating under the surface. It is this ...many people take to be their 'real' most innermost self – a terrifying idea, which naturally enough makes them feel they must stay concealed at all costs!" (p58)

Sometimes the emotions that are evoked are not the core problem instead the way we feel about having them, the resulting embarrassment and/or shame, often can be because shame is such a debilitating process. This debilitating process can be extremely painful as we feel that the negative parts of self have been uncomfortably exposed. Our actions and our thinking can be incapacitated.

Wurmser (1981) includes the following issues underlying the shame response;

1) I am weak and failing in competition; 2) I am dirty, messy - the content of myself is looked at with disdain and disgust; 3) I am defective - I have short-comings in my physical and mental makeup; and 4) I have lost control over my bodily functions and my feelings and self-exposing is dangerous and may be punished.

Given that a lot of individuals who seek help with substance misuse have experienced physical, emotional or sexual abuse or neglect, it is easy to see how these ideas might feature strongly in their sense of self.

The internalised critical voices which individuals hear in adulthood are echoes from the past that still influence how they behave in the present moment. A child who was told that he was lazy or stupid, for example, may still hear those voices in his head when he fails to understand an instruction or achieve a particular task in adulthood. While this internal critic plays a vital role in our socialisation, if it becomes too developed it promotes excessive shame. Erskine (1995) defines shame as:

> "a complex process involving: 1) a diminished self-concept, a lowering of one's self worth in confluence with the external humiliation and/or previously introjected criticism; 2) a defensive transposition of sadness and fear; and 3) a disavowal and retroflection of anger." (p109)

The shamed infant feels sadness about not being good enough in the eyes of the other and withdraws fearing abandonment because he feels he is not adequate and therefore not worthy of love. By withdrawing the infant is, at some level, abandoning the care-giver, but he can experience his action as that of being abandoned. It does not feel safe to be in touch with anger towards the primary care-giver when the infant is dependent on her/him for his survival. The anger cannot therefore be acknowledged and is turned in on the self. When this happens the infant gives away the need to be taken seriously, to be treated respectfully and does not understand that he has the ability to make an impact on another person.

Neil

> When Neil's partner destroyed his uniform, after Neil's initial terror had subsided, he was extremely upset and angry. Previously, Neil had been able to tell me that he was angry, but it was in a way where he

Addiction - This being human

seemed to merely mouth the words and stay detached from his bodily sensations. However, the retelling of this incident prompted Neil to express his anger to me in a manner that connected with his feelings.

After I had listened and empathised and while he was still emotionally aroused, I asked Neil to imagine his partner was sitting opposite him and to tell her how he felt. As he imagined her in the room, his posture became submissive and that of someone shamed. His voice became quiet and tentative as he apologised to her for not inviting her to the reunion. Even her imagined presence was too powerful, too overwhelming for him to stay in touch with. The anger was turned against himself, converted into self-criticism.

The way in which we adapt creatively to the circumstances in which we find ourselves can become a habitual way of being. If shame is experienced frequently, the defence against it becomes fixed and continues into adulthood. The adult treats as 'normal' not being taken seriously, being treated without respect and making no, or little, impact on others in relationship. This is not surprising, as for some it is or was normal and remains a true reflection of their lived experience.

Shame is a debilitating emotion we feel when someone we perceive as more powerful humiliates us and damages our self-esteem. The physical shrinking away from another is our way of being submissive. When an infant is shamed, he withdraws and so disrupts what Kaufmann (1985) calls 'the inter-personal bridge' between himself and the shamer. The psychological contact and the potential physical contact are broken. If this person is also the primary care-giver, the infant, by withdrawing from the critic, also puts himself out of reach of the potentially nurturing parent. He feels isolated, alone and vulnerable. As he retreats into his shell, it is as if he takes with him his own projection of how he imagined the other saw him. Erskine sees this as an attempt of the infant to hang on to a "semblance of a continuing relationship". (p109)

Evans (1994) proposes that in the absence of a relational other, the infant splits himself into two parts. The on-looking part, the 'I', then attacks and punishes the part of the infant that is being looked at – the 'me'. From this view point, self-harm can be seen as an acting out of self-loathing or self-contempt which has its roots in excessive infantile shame. Self-harming is facilitated by the body/mind split. It is the split that has gradually developed due to the infant's emotional needs not being met and the connection between the body and mind in the infant's lived experience not being validated.

The relationship with a substance mirrors the relationship with an abusing other. The individual desires the connection with the nurturing aspect of the drug when they are in emotional pain, as an infant would with the mother. People who drink excessively do so when their emotional needs are too great for them to manage on their own. They need to feel contained in that moment. Alcohol provides an instant solution. For many individuals experience has taught them that the relationship with others is unreliable and can lead to feelings of helplessness whereas picking up a drink is within their control. It blots out pain and therefore at some level can be perceived as effective and reliable.

However, although picking up the first drink is within their control, it is an illusion that drinking alcohol remains the way; the quantity of alcohol cannot be controlled by some-one who is physically addicted to it. It might appear to be within the control of the user and to be effective in the moment of the initial drink, but as the drinking continues the drinker experiences the alcohol as gaining control. The similarities between this 'here and now' experience of the relationship to the drink/drug and the 'there and then' relationship with his parents can trigger a transfer of his emotional response from what happened in the past to what is happening in the present. In other words, the individual can re-experience himself as he was in childhood; powerless, out of control, unable to rely on the one person, or substance, that he is dependent on.

When moments of clarity arrive, often the next morning, the drinker often wonders what happened while he was blacked out. He imagines what he might have said or done. He feels shame and humiliation; shame about his lack of control, shame about his alcohol-induced behaviour and often shame that he has let someone else down. He might then try to withdraw from the alcohol and decide to give up or curb the drinking. Or if he has given up hope and learnt from experience that he is unable to cut back or stop, he might feel anger and resentment, or more hopelessness and despair. As he retreats he takes with him negative and humiliating thoughts of what he imagines his colleagues, friends and others think of him. It is possible to see the use of a substance as an acting out of an unconscious wish for the individual's nurturing needs to be met in a reliable relationship.

Freud (1926) identified what he called 'the compulsion to repeat'. This refers to the idea that we unconsciously set up situations to mirror past experiences which have remained unresolved; it suggests that if a developmental phase has been missed, we unconsciously set up similar situations, in other words we repeat the situation with the unconscious hope that this time our needs will be met. You may have had the experience of going to your purse or wallet to pull out a ten pound note that you thought you had, to find it is not there. As you search the house, your jacket pockets, drawers and so on you find that you keep returning to your purse or wallet, even though logically you know the money is not in there. You might find it very difficult to settle, or think about anything else until you either find the money, or come to terms with the fact that it is gone forever; until this point it is unfinished business.

The normal process from dependence through independence to inter-dependence can be interrupted if it is not safe enough to be dependent on our primary care-giver. It is possible to see addiction as the consequence of this interruption. What is unfinished, what has not yet happened, is a nurturing relationship that can be trusted and relied on – becoming dependent on another. Instead this 'compulsion to repeat' is acted out in a destructive relationship with the substance and the initial trauma of not being held is continuing to be experienced. If we bear in mind the shame invoked by addictive behaviour, the behaviour can be seen as a continuous setting up and dashing of the hope to be seen, heard and met; a repeated destruction of the individual's eternal hope that he might depend on a reliable relationship and be held. It is deeply sad that this process is constantly re-enacted when a drug can never provide the consistent nurturing that is yearned for and required. Luckily, however, a human relationship that parallels the 'good-enough' mother can.

Erskine comments:

> "(The) defensive cycle of shame functions to maintain an illusion of attachment and loyalty to the person with whom the child was originally longing for an interpersonally contactful relationship." (p113)

Shame is nearly always experienced around the sense of failure that happens when a lapse occurs. The Cycle of Change identified by Prochaska, Diclemente and Norcross (1992) is particularly

Addiction - This being human

useful as an antidote to shame, as it normalises lapses. Rather than seeing recovery as a process which happens in a straight line, they propose that in order to change behaviour we need to go through a cycle, very often more than once. In the cycle they suggest, the client moves from pre-contemplation, to contemplation, to action, to maintenance, to lapse and then back to contemplation.

In pre-contemplation, the individual is using or drinking unaware that they are now using the substance to meet a need rather than drinking socially, or using drugs recreationally. Although they may have many problems in their lives related to their substance use, e.g. depression, anxiety, physical ailments, they do not yet fully acknowledge that their drug use is a direct consequence, or a contributory factor to their emotional condition, rather they tend to see their use as helpful in alleviating the negative symptoms.

The individual starts to think about, to contemplate, the problem when the evidence is so stark that it is no longer possible to stay in denial about the detrimental effect of the drug. At this stage, they might consider the problem and may or may not be ready to seek professional help, albeit just to talk about the problem. Once individuals have made a decision to change their behaviour, they have a reasonable amount of confidence to do it and it is a priority for them, they usually move into the action stage.

Here they start to cut down, or stop. If they are successful, maintaining their goals can at first seem easy, as they reap the benefits of their hard work. The high that some people feel initially is often described as similar to the quick fix of using their drug of choice. However, as time goes on, maintaining a low level of drink, methadone or maintaining abstinence can become arduous. The amount of work put in to achieving their goal remains similar, but the payback becomes less dramatic. It is frequently at this point that individuals will lapse.

When people who have internalised a lot of criticism lapse, it is easy for them to give up mentally as the internal chatter begins - "I am absolutely hopeless. I don't know why I ever thought I could give up… I am so weak-willed there is no point in me even trying. …I might just as well carry on drinking." However, if lapses can be seen as an integral part of the recovery process then they can become learning experiences. This new experience of not being criticised by the group or therapist, and of starting to see that mistakes are part of how we learn and develop, can in itself be healing.

Usually the physical and emotional consequences of a lapse are negative. The lapse can be a reminder of how chaotic and narrow their lives had become. If lapse is recognised as a normal process of change and the shame around it is not so intense, it is easier to return to contemplation and action. At this stage the circumstances around the lapse can be explored, so that they start to understand and become conscious of their triggers; the day of the week that it happened, whether this is regular pattern, whether they had mentally lapsed before they used or picked up a drink, what signals they might notice if that were to happen again, where they had been, what happened emotionally for them just before the lapse, who they were with and how they could have prevented it.

Once individuals start to understand the likely circumstances which cause them to lapse, they can start to anticipate dangerous situations and avoid them. As the Cycle of Change is repeated, so usually the previously unidentifiable triggers become conscious and can be dealt with, making lapses less likely. Portia Nelson's poem Autobiography in Five Short Chapters describes this process beautifully:

Addiction - This being human

Chapter I
I walk down the street.
There is a deep hole in the sidewalk
I fall in.
I am lost ... I am helpless.
It isn't my fault.
It takes forever to find a way out.

Chapter II
I walk down the same street.
There is a deep hole in the sidewalk.
I pretend I don't see it.
I fall in again.
I can't believe I am in the same place.
But, it isn't my fault.
It still takes a long time to get out.

Chapter III
I walk down the same street.
There is a deep hole in the sidewalk.
I see it is there.
I still fall in ... it's a habit ... but,
my eyes are open.
I know where I am.
It is my fault.
I get out immediately.

Chapter IV
I walk down the same street.
There is a deep hole in the sidewalk.
I walk around it.

Chapter V
I walk down another street.

This is a familiar story which resonates with most of us. It is useful to normalise the perseverance it takes to change habitual behaviour as this helps to diminish the shame about lapses.

Danny

When Danny came for help, he was drinking a bottle of vodka a day. He had been for some one-to-one counselling but had found it unhelpful, probably because he had gone there to please his partner and had not been really committed to the process. Over the course of a few weeks, Danny gradually cut back until he was abstinent. He found that he could maintain this for about a week and then he would have half a bottle of vodka. Each time we reminded Danny about the Cycle of Change and normalised his lapse. Danny learnt from each lapse. He started to notice a link between them and the contact he was having with his ex-girlfriend along with one or two other situations, in which he had trouble containing his emotions.

Then, very uncharacteristically, Danny did not appear for about four days. He left a message on an answerphone to say he was OK and that he would be back in soon. When he did come in, he had the remnants of a black eye. He told the group that he was feeling "like a complete idiot" and "shit". His internal critic was much in evidence as he repeatedly chastised himself and his body language spoke of the shame he was feeling. He explained that he had lapsed, but this time the amount he drank had been unlimited. He had become aggressive and had got into a physical fight with his brother.

The group reminded Danny about the Cycle of Change, but this time due to the amount of shame Danny was experiencing, he found it difficult to hear what they were saying, to relate it to himself and take in the support offered.

Addiction - This being human

Yontef (1993) comments that the sanction for guilt is punishment and that the sanction for shame is abandonment. In not turning up to the group we might interpret Danny's behaviour as an acting out of guilt and shame. In terms of relational need we might also think about his actions as self-punishment; isolating himself and abandoning the group as a defence against being abandoned by them. Danny's absenting behaviour when a lapse occurred is a very common event amongst individuals who use substances to self-soothe, which sadly denies support and nurturing when most needed.

If lapse is not understood as a normal part of the process involved in behaviour change, it is easy to see each lapse as a failure. When this is the case, it can lead to feelings of helplessness, defeat and hopelessness that turn attempting to get clean or dry into an insurmountable task which can result in the giving up of all hope. It is more encouraging to look on each lapse as a learning opportunity just as inventors keep repeating experiments until their goal is achieved. It is also useful for individuals to understand that there is a correlation between the intensity of the emotions triggered and the likelihood of a lapse.

> Tim
>
> Tim was experiencing a lot of shame about that fact that he had had two lapses close together. However, he managed to return to the group to tell them about the most recent trigger. He had returned home after walking the dog to be confronted by his partner. She attacked him verbally about an e-mail message he had received. It had been from a female member of a religious organisation that had been trying to support Tim in dealing with family issues. They had been corresponding for several months and it ended

> with "lots of love". His partner accused him of being unfaithful. She had entered his personal space and was throwing her arms around. Tim left the house and went to the pub to get a drink.
>
> Tim had previously been the victim of domestic violence, which had resulted in severe injury. Remembering this fact, the group pointed out how terrifying the recent experience must have been. Tim could then contact his feelings about how life threatening the situation had felt in the moment as past memories came flooding back. He could then see how he had resorted to his old behaviour of drinking to cope with *extremely* overwhelming feelings. Thereafter he was able to be less self-critical and more accepting of this lapse.

We can tell intuitively that some individuals carry excessive amounts of shame because of their body language. They often give little eye contact, sit hunched over and find it difficult, or impossible to speak in the group. Their fear of being seen or heard is so high because they believe that when people really find out who they are they will be shocked, disgusted and will withdraw. Shame however, is sometimes more difficult to detect. Given this, it is a good precautionary move to explain the Cycle of Change to all individuals using substances to cope with their emotions, before a probable lapse, so as to pre-empt a full-blown relapse. If this information is not provided then the client is more likely to retreat in shame and to disengage with the agency or therapist if or when a lapse occurs. Moreover, any client who holds a lot of *intrinsic* shame might rupture the 'interpersonal bridge' permanently and leave treatment.

Once clients can see that to change any behaviour is very difficult, they can appreciate and respect the even harder task of recovery, given the added complication of a habit involving an addictive substance. The example of driving on the Continent can be useful. Before we leave England we prepare our cars and our minds for driving on the right-hand side of the road. As we leave the ferry the road signs remind us to stay on the right and we confidently drive on the right-hand side of the road, until we pull off for a break or become distracted. When we pull back onto the road, unless we are vigilant, it is easy to slip back into automatic pilot and start driving dangerously on the left-hand side. The more we travel safely on the right, the easier it becomes to maintain. When individuals understand that all habitual behaviours are difficult to change, they can begin to appreciate that lapses are part of being human and find it easier to forgive themselves and others.

Working to gradually diminish an individual's intrinsic shame is a long process. Describing the origin of shame, Yontef comments that it;

> "(D)evelops in an environmental context in which the child does not receive a sense of being known, accepted, loved and respected for being who he or she is, including "deficits" (p.493).

It follows that what is needed to diminish and eradicate shame is an environment where these needs are met. Evans adds that to work with shame we need to be *in an equal relationship with the individual*, rather than one of power.

If we are to be non-judgemental, individuals need to be met at the place where they are on their journey of recovery. This can be frustrating for anyone working in the field who knows that a particular person will not be able to control their alcohol intake yet their chosen goal is reduction and control, rather than abstinence. Usually at the beginning, if someone has been using alcohol as a way of coping with their feelings, they find the thought of never drinking again very threatening. Alcohol is often referred to as 'my best friend' and can be the only thing in their lives that has recently been experienced as helpful.

Although some individuals might initially need the constraint of a total abstinence recovery programme, if we insist that total abstinence is the *only* way for *all* individuals, we are exercising power to assert our wishes, however well-intentioned, on to another. There are many different routes in recovery. People need choice, and individuals will intuitively know the best way forward for their own personal circumstances. Enforced abstinence, when it is not asked for, holds the potential to re-create an emotionally distressing situation for the person seeking help, as the power dynamic and coercion can mirror their previous, often abusive, relationships. In such circumstances then, however well-intentioned the professionals involved are, it is likely that they could be re-experienced as the bullies or the abusers from the past. If abstinence is insisted on, against the wishes of the individual, then they are being asked to ignore their body 'felt sense' of what is, or is not, comfortable and safe. Such action encourages and perpetuates the body/mind split, rather than heals it. If the individual does nevertheless go against his own instincts, it will be the critical, punitive part of him that will help him to maintain his sobriety – the very same part that keeps his self-care and nurturing side of self at bay. Ultimately, it is the integration of the mind and body, and the encouragement of the nurturing part of the self that can ensure long-term sobriety.

While it is possible to sustain other people's chosen goals over our own, we do not feel satisfied by such action – it is out of tune with our preferences and needs. This can eventually generate resentment which when it builds up can become the trigger for a lapse. Individuals often identify the 'Sod it!' factor

Addiction - This being human

at the moment a lapse occurs. Any insistence on abstinence gives the drinker the unconscious message that the drinking part of them is unacceptable; once again the 'deficit' part of them is rejected and our opportunity to provide a truly *reparative* relationship is missed.

Commenting on the Paradoxical Theory of Change, Beisser (1970) states that if we push someone towards change, they will resist it. On the other hand, if we help them to be emotionally present where they are, they will work whole-heartedly to achieve it:

> "Change does not take place through a coercive attempt by the individual or by another person to change him, but it does take place if one takes the time and effort to be what he is – *to be fully invested in his current position.* Change occurs when one becomes what he is, not when he becomes what he is not. ...To heal suffering one must first experience it to the full." (p63).

Once people are more in tune with their bodies, and have learnt to regulate their emotional states in a healthy way rather than by using substances, they can really be in touch with their current situations; once they are not in denial, can be emotionally in the present moment, respond rather than react, then they will usually choose abstinence over controlled drinking naturally. To be in the here-and-now, we need to know which emotions are current and which emotions are simply echoes of the past.

An attitude of non-judgement, empathy and respect can be amplified in a supportive group where everyone feels they have a place to be heard and seen. They are able to risk exposing more of their inner processes as these feelings are normalised and found to be acceptable to their peers, as well as trained professionals who are "paid to say nice things". The weight of the group members' encouragement and empathic comments can intensify and speed up the experience of being both accepted, and acceptable, as the evidence to that effect for each individual becomes overwhelming.

As an individual gains a greater sense of self, they can gradually acquire a sense of the other and distinguish between the victim of shame; themselves, and the person acting in a shaming way; the abuser. For the individual to relate to themselves as the innocent baby, or child, can be very powerful.

Harry

Harry had a very difficult relationship with his mother, who was highly critical and constantly blamed him for anything that went wrong within the family. When he came into counselling, he had little contact with his parents. His self-esteem was very low and he found it difficult to hear good comments about himself. He thought of himself as intrinsically 'clumsy' and 'bad' and saw his mother as 'wise' and 'good'.

As Harry had been growing up, his mother had repeatedly told him that he had been a "nightmare baby". We explored what those words could have meant. Holding on to the notion of the innocent baby, he was able to see that "nightmare" must have referred to his behaviour, rather than his being. Harry was gradually able to see that he had not been born inherently 'bad'. He was able to make the link between his early experiences in relationship with his critical mother and his low self-esteem, to see his life story in perspective and to understand that his mother's behaviour and comments might have originated, at least in part, from her own distress, rather than from his own 'badness'. This allowed him to be more self-compassionate and eventually curb his self-harming behaviours.

Generally, when individuals understand the normal function of shame, the origin of their excessive shame and how it affects their lives in the present moment, it becomes possible to gain both conscious awareness and therefore control over it. Providing the language for individuals to identify their own shame process and working out its current triggers is useful to curb the potential for cycles to repeat.

Kaufmann (1985) brings our attention to the defences against shame which protect us from further exposure. He includes contempt, rage, striving for power, for perfection, internal withdrawal and the transfer of blame. Rage, contempt and internal withdrawal work by keeping others at a distance, so that the self cannot be exposed, whereas striving for power and perfection are strategies which try to compensate for the feelings of inadequacy.

Once shame has begun to be felt, one of the main defences is to transfer the blame for the incident onto something external. For example, if we are ashamed because we have lapsed, for example, to blame our partner for provoking a row shifts alleviates us from the responsibility. However, at the same time the consequence of ridding us of responsibility is that we have no perceived control over our action to drink. Kaufmann sums up how this blaming process debilitates us further:

> "And when blaming becomes sufficiently directed outside oneself, that is externalized, we may see an individual who perceives the source of all that goes wrong to lie outside the self, and, paradoxically, beyond internal control. And although that individual

> resents the resulting feeling of powerlessness, a powerlessness to affect and change what ails him, he never recognizes that he has colluded in the very process of creating that powerlessness." (p92)

It is a testament to the human spirit that hope can often be held on to, despite all the evidence, as addiction infuses us with a profound and powerful sense of powerlessness.

Bessel van Kolk et al (1996) comment that shame is:

> "(C)ritical to understanding the lack of self-regulation in trauma victims and the capacity of the abused persons to become abusers. Trauma is usually accompanied by intense feelings of humiliation; to feel threatened, helpless and out of control is a vital attack on the capacity to count on oneself. Shame is the emotion related to having let oneself down. The shame that accompanies such personal violations as rape, torture and abuse is so painful that it is frequently dissociated: victims may be unaware of its presence, and yet it comes to dominate their interactions with the environment." (p75)

In the same way that the shame process is prevalent and yet often unconscious amongst our client group, so it might be prevalent and unconscious amongst those who work in the addiction field. If we bear in mind the defences against shame: contempt, rage, striving for power, for perfection, internal withdrawal and the transfer of blame, then as professionals working in the field we can monitor our own potential acting-out.

For professionals, understanding shame is central to understanding self-harming behaviours. It allows us to understand the frightening, helpless and vulnerable position of a dependent infant, who acts creatively to survive in a hostile environment, and who, in so doing, cuts himself off from the person he is dependent on for his survival and ability to thrive. It allows us to understand why individuals who come for help around addictive substances do not initially accept responsibility for their actions. Once they can appreciate that they are not being judged, their shame becomes diminished, then they will be able to take responsibility for their actions and move more easily along the recovery path.

Many individuals who use alcohol or drugs to cope with their emotions can be seen as the shamed child grown into their adult skin. When shame is held in mind we can understand why so many we work with disengage temporarily or permanently from treatment. The shaming behaviour that is acted out by using a substance can point to the unconscious wish for a reparative relationship: a relationship that can be provided in treatment once we become aware of its need.

Further reading:

CLARKSON P. (1989) *Gestalt Counselling in Action.* London: Sage Publications.

KAUFMANN G. (1985) *Shame: the power of caring.* Cambridge, Mass: Schenkman Books.

NATHANSON D.L. (1992) *Shame and Pride. Affect, sex and the birth of the self.* New York: W.W. Norton and Co.

WURMER L, (1981) *The Mask of Shame.* Baltimore: John Hopkins University Press

> The time will come
> when, with elation
> you will greet yourself arriving
> at your own door, in your own mirror
> and each will smile at the other's welcome.
> ~Derek Walcot

> If we don't tell our stories, our stories tell us
> ~Stephen Grosz

What follows in the next two chapters are two individual accounts of lived experience. I have changed some of the factual details so that the individuals concerned cannot be identified, but the story of their experience in terms of their inner world has not been changed.

Although these are only the narratives of two individuals, the issues they present will resonate with many people who use substances to deal with their emotions. These narratives illustrate the issues which present themselves repeatedly within treatment - the social isolation, the shame, the lack of a sense of self, the difficulty of expressing emotions, low self-esteem, suppressed anger, split-off parts of self and the difficulty in taking decisions.

7

KEVIN'S STORY

> Nobody heard him, the dead man,
> But still he lay moaning:
> I was much further out than you thought
> And not waving but drowning.
> ~Stevie Smith

Kevin, aged 44, worked part-time as a vicar and part-time as a teacher of English at a local college. He was referred to me by his doctor. The doctor cited depression as the main reason for the referral and further commented "He feels quite socially isolated and has difficulties making real friends. He finds that he is using alcohol to make up for this and is drinking about 60 units a week". The doctor asked if he could be seen as soon as possible and added, "He bravely told me about his long-term alcohol problem and was so relieved to be taken seriously and offered help. I feel we should really grasp the situation while he is motivated to seek help." At this stage, I noted that Kevin was probably someone who did not expect to be taken seriously and wondered what the relationship had been like with his primary carer.

Kevin remembered his childhood as being very lonely. He

told me that his mother had had severe post-natal depression. His main companion was the family cat. This did not change when he went to school. At first he attended the village school, but he was teased so badly that his parents moved him. At this second primary school Kevin remembered creating a fantasy world to live in, and told me that he had occasionally involved other pupils in this world.

Kevin often presented a very punitive and strict side of himself. He told me that he had become like this in an attempt to win his mother's love. He felt that if he tried harder and was stricter with himself, she would eventually love him. A few weeks into our work he came to realise that this firm control was partly what was causing him stress and anxiety, whereas he had previously thought it was what was needed in order to reduce his stress levels. After discussing the punitive voice in his head, Kevin started to notice it more. He tried to just notice it when it appeared and not to be drawn into it.

Kevin found mixing with people in any social setting difficult. He had high levels of social anxiety. He felt that if he did not watch himself he had a tendency to "butt in" and he felt that his real, spontaneous self was not acceptable. Kevin commented that he 'talked too much', not just with me but in all his relationships. He realised that if there was a silent gap in the conversation he felt uncomfortable, as though he was 'failing' and that he needed to 'perform'. We wondered about the silence that he might have endured as an infant when his mother was unable to attend to his needs.

He explained that he had no friends and that his only social contact now was in his two jobs and that he did not know how to be with people when there was no prescribed activity. His roles kept him safe in relationships, in that the roles he held dictated the way that he should be with his pupils and with members of his congregation. Early on in our work together, he commented on feeling 'a degree of satisfaction' at being able to leave acquaintances behind whenever he changed parish.

Talking about his parent's relationship he told me that they often had rows. Frequently his mother's criticisms of his father would prompt fights. He described how frightened he had felt when this happened. He likened his experience to 'melting chocolate'. He remembered trying to calm them down and being told it was none of his business and so he was left feeling helpless and powerless in the face of what seemed to him to be a disintegration of the family and himself. I could see clearly Kevin playing the role of rescuer and linked this in my mind to the Drama Triangle.

Kevin described his adolescent years as 'terrifying'. He woke frequently with nightmares and felt as though he was choking. He explained that he found this period of his life so stressful because he feared leaving home, although he did eventually go to university.

During the session he often curled his shoulders over as if to protect himself. He talked in a factual way emphasising the phrases he thought important with little facial expression. He repeated himself often, using slightly different phrases and expressions each time, as though he was trying to make a really difficult concept clear. I thought about his previous experience of not being heard and how his current repetition might signify him trying to pre-empt my not hearing or understanding him. At the same time it often felt as if he was not expecting a response from me. I was struck that the way he addressed me was similar to the way in which a teacher might address a class. It seemed to be one-sided in direction. The way he related to me helped me to think about how he might have been related to by his mother and how he was relating to others outside of our sessions.

The language Kevin used in our first few sessions was unusual. There were lots of religious overtones: "mercifully", "miraculously and "by God's mercy". In context, these words conveyed a sense of helplessness, as though his experience of himself was one of powerlessness and as though he was reliant on an outside force. I thought again about the Drama Triangle, and noted how these phrases reflected Kevin's vision of himself as a victim, unable to demonstrate self-agency.

Several themes emerged as Kevin talked about his past and current relationships. First he experienced himself as "abusive" in relationships. He told me about his "abuse" of his school friends and work colleagues. By "abuse" he explained that he meant that he involved them in his fantasies. Secondly, he frequently seemed to experience others as "opinionated". This had been how he had experienced his previous counsellor. He told me that his boss was "someone who always had to be right". He also reported that he had trouble marking some of the essays written by students who held strong views.

Since it was his usual experience of relationships, I wondered whether he was worried about 'abusing' me and if he would ultimately experience me as 'opinionated'. By this stage I realised that, to prevent him from disengaging, I was going to have to watch out for this negative way of seeing others. I would need to bring it into his conscious awareness by talking about it, if this tendency was not going to undermine his relationship with me. If I did not bring out the pattern of perceiving others in this way, I thought it likely that he might terminate therapy when he started to experience me in that way.

During our first session I experienced Kevin as detached and self-contained. The image that sprang to mind was that of a stuffed animal in a glass show case. I noted that when he left the room, I shook his hand. As I had never done this before with any client I had to wonder why. I came to the conclusion that it had been an act borne out of my frustration at being kept at a distance. I considered the handshake to be an acting out on my part in response to his detachment. It was my way of making sure that we had some kind of contact. It was very interesting to note how my frustration had manifested itself in such a socially acceptable way; as a handshake. This seemed to mirror closely Kevin's anger hidden behind the socially acceptable behaviour of a vicar and a teacher.

Later Kevin told me that his mother had never been able to acknowledge his pain. Straight after his birth she had suffered from post-natal depression. When Kevin was older, if he fell over or hurt himself he was told not to make a fuss. Likewise, when he cried out in the night, struggling to deal with a nightmare, he was told not to cry 'Wolf'. I was able to link Kevin's current expectations of not being heard or taken seriously, to his mother's inability to hear his pain and act on it.

Even in these first few sessions, I could tell that I was experienced by Kevin in two different ways – as the idealised mother who could do no wrong and the mother who was critical and unresponsive. He wanted desperately for me to like him and he told me so. I noted how he tried to please me by agreeing with all my interventions without giving them much thought. In the same breath, he told me that he did not expect me to like him and he experienced any silence between us as me being hostile and made lots of references to not being liked by others.

In the room Kevin related to me much as a child would an

adult, although I was not conscious of this in the beginning. Between the fourth and fifth session I needed to contact Kevin and was shocked by how different he was on the phone. He spoke to *me* as though I was a child. When we explored this apparent shifting imbalance in our relationship he commented that he had never really related to anyone as an equal. In his childhood, he only related to his parents and his sister; he had little experience of relating to his peers.

Early on we looked at what alcohol had meant to Kevin. It made him feel 'included', not only because his grandparents had given it to him but also because he had received the message from his parents that he was "grown up" if he drank. His mother took Guinness as a tonic when she was pregnant and so Kevin thought of it as "medicinal" and "safe". He had started to drink heavily at university. Alcoholic beverages seemed to act as a transitional object for him; an object that helped him to feel safe when he was away from his mother. This exploration brought the realisation that social isolation and loneliness were big triggers for his drinking and helped him to acknowledge his ambivalent feelings about alcohol.

Often Kevin talked about what he called the "cycle of alcohol abuse". How he would drink to feel better until remorse would set in and he would be unable to hold on to the idea of himself as a "good" person. As he told me this I had a visual image of the Drama Triangle in my head and I could see the alcohol slide from the rescuer to the persecutor position

After six weeks Kevin had begun to reduce his intake of alcohol and was starting to reap the physical and psychological rewards. However, he noticed how he now found it difficult to believe that this state of affairs could last. He also mentioned his ambivalent feelings towards our relationship. He felt that there was some shame attached to the fact that he was coming to rely on me. Yet at the same time he talked of his relief at having some support.

Around this time Kevin was able to talk about how he felt like an infant abandoned on a doorstep. He was fearful that I might not be able to cope with the strength of his emotions. He felt foolish that the past was having such an effect on his current life and fearful of the future. He felt apart from the rest of society and "odd" because his behaviour was often "inappropriate". He explained that he often felt "at sea", not knowing the difference between reality and fantasy, especially in relation to his feelings. He started to question whether his own barometer of emotional and physical distress was out of alignment with the rest of humanity. We related this to his mother's denial of his feelings.

Our first break came after two months. On our recommencement of the sessions, one theme of his narrative revolved around people not being there for him and he became very upset. He gave examples of his sister, his students, a friend and even one of his cats which had wandered off. He felt that 'everything was out of control' and he felt 'abandoned'. At this point he was out of touch with his anger, towards others for not being there for him and towards me for leaving him, but could contact his feelings of sadness. It was interesting that this suppressed anger was acted out by depriving himself of a planned break.

He had planned to go on several day trips that week with a friend, but told me that he was now 'unable to go'. Then immediately after those comments he started to talk about his 'punitive' mother. I wondered about the internalised punitive mother that stopped him now from taking a few days off work. It seemed that, on some level, he felt that he had been responsible for the abandonment and that, as it had been his fault, he needed to be punished.

Soon after that incident, he began to talk about his early experience of anger. He related how he felt his anger might harm anyone at whom it was directed, if they were vulnerable and how it might catapult and return to hurt him if they were strong.

Gradually, as the sessions progressed, Kevin came to understand that many of his current behaviours, his relationship with food, alcohol and prescribed medication, his inability to sustain relationships and enjoy leisure activities, were a consequence of his early infant experience. He came to a realisation that what he had felt as 'loneliness', 'hunger' and as 'a void inside him' were all related in some way to how his nurturing needs had not been met. This 'hole' that he experienced inside himself and his own attempts to fill it became another recurring theme.

Kevin increasingly experienced himself as consisting of two major parts which he called the 'head' and the 'gut'. I thought of this in terms of a body/mind split. Much of his narrative was about the dynamic between these two parts of himself and how he was trying to be more in touch with his 'gut' and less influenced by his 'head'. He explained that his gut wanted to be sad, alone and peaceful but that his head told him to snap out of it" and not to be "so self-indulgent!" He recognised the latter as an echo from his mother.

Kevin at this point was drinking much less, was starting to eat more healthily and was trying to listen more to what he wanted to do rather than what he felt he ought to do. I praised him for his achievements. He became silent. I wondered whether my comments were too at odds with his own self-image for him to take them in. When I questioned what was going on for him at that moment, he told me that he had experienced my praise as how his mother would have reacted: I had chosen to focus on something positive, rather than highlight his emotional pain.

Addiction - This being human

This insight reminded him how his parents had always praised him for even the smallest academic achievement but failed to respond to even the most obvious and loud signals of his emotional distress. I realised that unwittingly I had repeated the pattern in that moment.

At about three months into our work, Kevin said that he felt "much better" and that now he could see the "light at the end of the tunnel". He provided me with lots of examples of how he had managed to listen to his gut more and to act on it. He intimated that our sessions could come to an end.

The feelings I picked up from him were those of joy tinged with doubt. I mentioned the doubt and wondered with him about a flight into health - whether he was really better, or whether for some unconscious reason he felt he should be better. As we explored what was going on for him, it emerged that the previous counsellor had ended their sessions together around the four month period. We thought about his decision to end the therapy in terms of a body memory of being abandoned by his previous counsellor. His unconscious was prompting him to leave the relationship with me before I had the opportunity to leave him. In this way, his unconscious was trying to help him to anticipate and avoid a recurrence of feeling the painful emotions brought up by his initial abandonment by his mother. We agreed to continue working together.

After this session, Kevin returned to the theme of being "lost and confused", commenting that he could not work out what path he was on. He talked about the difficulty of sustaining relationships and how, if there was no agenda at a social gathering, he felt "laughed at, ignored, passed over, attacked or rejected". He told me that he found these situations "life-threateningly stressful" and went on to recount how in out-of-role relationships he allowed himself to be used and then felt justified in ending the relationship.

He described that as a child he had "manipulated plastic soldiers around a rockery". I noted the word "manipulated" and its impact on my body. It felt as though Kevin was being very harsh and critical about his actions. I wondered if Kevin was telling me that he now felt lost in relationship with me. His script was missing. It was as if his role as client had come to an end, at some level, the previous week when he claimed to be better and now he had little idea how to sustain our relationship. I wondered whether he was experiencing me as a cruel, neglectful mother and whether he felt passed over and ignored in our silences together. We talked it through, linking it to his early experience again and his lack of a meaningful relationship with his depressed mother and his peers.

Around this time Kevin related that an ex-girlfriend had suddenly appeared in his life her husband had just died and she had turned to him for comfort. He explained how he felt 'trapped by brambles' when anyone needed to rely on him and he became tearful as he added 'it means you're needed'. I wondered if he thought I felt trapped by brambles as he was now relying on me. I was also reminded about his recent decision to try and end the therapy and wondered if this had been partly to do with his anxiety about becoming dependent on me.

Kevin came to realise that he felt unable to show his anger towards me. He explained that it was too scary to think of me as lacking in some or in any way, when he felt he relied on me so heavily. We related this to his early experience with his mother and how it must have felt very scary to be angry with someone on whom you were also dependent. He could see too how this influenced his current relationships, not only with me but also with his boss, his mother and with God.

Soon afterwards Kevin relayed how a part of him felt as though he did not exist and how nothing he did seemed to have an impact on the environment or others. He brought up an incident that happened at work. He told me that about two weeks previously a colleague at work complaining of a headache had received lots of sympathy and a suggestion was made that he go home. Kevin had made a similar complaint about having a headache this week but felt "no-one had taken any notice". He was distressed and puzzled by the contrast. By linking it to his childhood experience of his mother never taking his pain seriously, Kevin came to see that he still anticipated not being taken seriously. We talked about the way he told his colleague that he had a headache – the tone of voice he used, the actual words, his timing and so on. We wondered if his not being taken seriously had become a self-fulfilling prophecy because, at some level, he did not take his own pain seriously. It was as if this was being communicated to colleagues unconsciously, so they did not take him seriously either. We thought of this in terms of Kevin projecting his expectations onto his colleagues.

Kevin often talked about not really knowing "what was real and what was not real" and so he found it difficult to make decisions. He made a link between his not being explicit about his needs and why he eventually experienced all relationships as taking him "for granted" and "taking advantage of him".

Looking at his relationships generally, Kevin commented that he saw them in terms of a power struggle because of the conflict he had witnessed between his parents. He commented that he felt "naked" out of role and that he related to my role as a therapist rather than to me as a person. He said he sometimes experienced me like an object, and he gave the example of a telephone. I noted a telephone was an inanimate object which brought to mind the plastic soldiers on the rockery. He commented that it was only his cats with whom he felt relaxed and trusting.

At some point during our work together, Kevin lost one of his cats. He was very tearful. It reminded him that his attachment to cats was stronger than his attachment to people. He felt that he was in the grieving process for the cat, but that he was also grieving at his realisation that he had little real human contact in his life. He told me he had needed to have a drink, as it was the only way he could cope with his distress.

Shortly afterwards, Kevin came into one session in a highly agitated state. He told me that the "whole of his college was up in arms" about an inappropriate remark he had made in the college newsletter. Kevin thought that as a consequence he might lose his job; he might need to move out of the district, which would mean that he would be able to see me anymore. He was distraught and told me that he had been attacked "in a very calm, gentle way" by another member of staff. He commented that "if somebody who was not an English speaker had witnessed the scene, they would not have guessed I was being attacked".

When we explored what had actually happened it turned out that he had written a light-hearted article about spring and had used the word "copulating". I was able to point out that only *one* person had made a comment. I was able to let him know that I did not find "copulating" offensive and I suggested that maybe others had not been offended either. I noted how quickly his stable world dissolved beneath his feet, how exposed he had felt and how his all-or-nothing thinking had spiralled downwards with a devastating effect on his mental and emotional state.

Addiction - This being human

I linked his distress to his early experience with his mother and we thought about his lack of an internalised safe base, or supporting other. In the session, however, I was able to provide an experience of a supporting other, by not being drawn into his distress and yet at the same time empathising with it. I was able to contain him. Kevin left the session feeling confident that the situation would 'blow over'. From this experience and others like it Kevin was able to see that his extreme mood swings were to do with his inner world and not exclusively to do with what was actually happening in the outer world.

Later Kevin noted that he often enjoyed breaking stereotypes because his mother saw everything in such "black and white" terms. He thought that on some level, he was getting at his mother and it gave him great pleasure to do behave out of character for the role that he was in at the time, just like swearing while in his vicar role.

During one particular session Kevin noted that when his reality was not acknowledged by others it felt as though the floor beneath him fell away. He described it as "falling into a pit". He commented how the death of his cat, being given more responsibility at work and his physical health had not been acknowledged by anyone other than me. Again we linked this to his expectation of not being heard or listened to and how this might affect his communication with others. He wondered how he could get the balance right between being heard and being "too over the top". We considered how he might take his own bodily sensations and emotions more seriously.

As the Christmas holidays approached Kevin became upset. The holidays reminded him that our relationship was 'purely professional'. He told me that I was looking ill and that he was concerned about my health. He was experiencing me as if I was the mother for whom he was too much and he seemed to take on the responsibility for my perceived state of ill health. I picked up his desperation and also his anger. I noted that this time I could feel the anger, unlike in our first session.

By this stage, Kevin had stopped drinking, but he still had an occasional lapse when events seemed too difficult for him to manage. Shortly after one such lapse Kevin started to question his progress in therapy. He told me that he needed to know that it was working. When I could not provide him with the reassurance that he needed, he told me he was grateful for the many insights he had gained, but that he needed more than this. He told me that a part of him thought that I was useless, although another part was sorry for not being more appreciative, after all I had done for him. I questioned again whether he thought he might be experiencing me as if I was his mother. I felt I was split into the mother who could get nothing right and the mother who had done a lot for him.

A few weeks later, I arrived ten minutes early for our session, but after Kevin. The receptionist had told him that he did not think that I was working that day. When Kevin came into the room he began by telling me how he thought he must have got it wrong and immediately started to express self-doubt. He then went on to criticise himself as a vicar. He commented that he was not "really sure how good he was". He told me that "it was a job in which it was very difficult to judge whether one was having an impact or not". These comments were contrary to Kevin's usual comments about himself as a vicar, because he usually thought of himself as good at his job, so I asked whether he was also, at some level, talking about me and having these thoughts because of the muddle about whether I was there or not.

Kevin agreed that actually he was angry with me, but that he had needed to take the blame himself. This was the first time that Kevin actually experienced his anger, or could acknowledge the anger he sometimes felt towards me. We thought about his need to take on the blame rather than blame the other. He described how as a child he had taken on the blame for his father's behaviour by lying to the mother in order to protect his father from his mother's wrath.

As our work together progressed, Kevin told me that he was letting go of the previous image he had retained of his mother as perfect and as someone who only experienced the occasional hiccup in her parental care-giving role. He said he was coming to a new understanding of his mother as someone who, because of her own pain, had to do anything to hold onto her own self-image as a caring mother. He saw his mother as someone who hid herself behind a protective shield, so that nothing could dent, or hurt this image. He found this realisation very painful and reiterated his sense that he felt he was grieving for the loss of the "perfect" mother. Kevin added that although this was painful he felt that he now saw his mother in a more realistic and coherent way.

As his image of the perfect mother subsided, Kevin questioned and expressed some confusion about whether it had been him, his mother or both of them that had "manipulated and abused" others. I noted the real confusion for him about what belonged to his mother and what belonged to him. Previously he had commented "If I am strict enough, conform enough and am good enough, maybe my mum will accept me". It followed from his new image of his mother that there was little realistic hope of his pain and needs ever being met or acknowledged by his mother, no matter what he did. We discussed whether he might in time be able to acknowledge and fulfil his needs genuinely for himself.

Kevin noted similarities between how he used drink now and

how he had used fantasy as a child with his classmates. Both the drinking and the creating of fantasies induced guilt and shame, both provided the terror that he would be found out, both were felt to be compulsive and part of him was always on the brink of giving up the behaviours.

One day Kevin arrived distressed and told me that he had noticed a cat lying at the side of the road abandoned. He realised that he felt so upset because he could identify with it. He then talked of his ambivalence about wanting to be seen and heard; he noted how safe it felt staying invisible and silent and yet how frustrated it made him feel at the same time. He talked about the conflict between him wanting support and how difficult he found it to ask for it. We wondered together about how he kept himself invisible and silent. Kevin noticed that one way he made himself unobtrusive was by choosing to dress in a mundane way, so as not to attract attention to himself.

About eight months into the work, I explained to Kevin that I would be taking a summer break in a month's time. In the following few sessions he talked about how he was feeling "near to the edge", "on the edge of a precipice" and "about to fall off". He spoke of his fear of being caught in a gradual emotional and mental decline which would lead to complete annihilation. We linked the feelings prompted by his expected experience of the two-week break from me - at a time when he was feeling dependent on me - with his experience as a baby and his past abandonment.

In the next session, he told me that he had been to see the doctor, who had offered him some anti-depressants and advised a two-week break from work. I noted how he had turned towards medication to support himself during my absence. He asked for my advice about whether he should take the tablets or not. He told me he did not want to take them if they would interfere with the counselling, because he knew that "this was the solution" to his problem. He commented that he was very clever at hiding his depression from his students and parishioners. I pointed out that other people could not validate his feelings and offer their support if he did not register his feelings with them. We discussed his fears about letting others know who he really was.

Kevin spent several weeks exploring the lack of structure in his life and how this was linked in some way to his ability to be motivated. We looked at it in terms of self-care. During these weeks, he came to a realisation that sometimes he was happier to set himself up to fail, rather than live with uncertainty. We were able to link this to his 'opinionated' mother who was herself unable to deal with uncertainty.

Kevin told me about an incident in the parish when he was overwhelmed by negative emotions. He was cross with himself and was self-critical. In this session he was able to make the link between his rejection of his needy part and his mother's rejection of his needy baby-self.

On returning from a holiday that he had spent with his mother, Kevin confirmed that whatever he said or did in that relationship had little effect. He cited various incidents where he had asked for or suggested something and how she had not listened. He also recounted how several times his mother had suggested that she knew what was best for him and insisted that this was what he really needed. When he suggested a day trip to one place, she proposed that he would much prefer another destination. When he asked for his food to be cooked slightly differently, he was told her way was more nutritious. Although a part of him understood that she had done her best to nurture him, given her depression, another part of him was furious with her. He was now in touch with his anger and knew that it was his mother that he was angry with.

Ten months into our work together, Kevin told me he was angry with me because he had drunk too much at the weekend. He had experienced a surge of "surplus energy", but had felt "gagged" and had paced the room for a while before opening a bottle of cider. A part of him wanted to take the blame himself, or to blame the process of counselling, but another part was angry with me for not "fixing it". We talked it through and he came to see how he experienced both the alcohol and me as both having the potential to support him, but ultimately both letting him down in the same way that his mother had. I noted, however, that he was now able to feel anger, locate the source of it - me - and tell me so. Kevin was now able to reclaim his anger.

By the time we had been working together for about fifteen months, Kevin was approached and offered a job in another parish. Over the following weeks, as he considered taking the job, he commented that if he decided to move this time it would feel different. He realised for the first time that he was going to miss some of his parishioners. He told me that he felt "upset" and "overjoyed" by this discovery: upset because he would genuinely miss someone for the first time and overjoyed because it said something about the quality of the relationship he had had with them.

As our work came to an end, Kevin commented that he felt that he now had more control in his relationship with his boss, with me and with his use of alcohol. Reflecting back, Kevin commented that he was not continually tearful anymore and that he had become much happier with his own company. He was feeling less ambivalent about "people being there" for him. He remained slightly anxious that this better frame of mind might not last forever, but he was on the whole more confident and felt much more stable in his everyday life.

He now found the thought of drink physically repellent and he had started to attend AA meetings regularly. Kevin also had ambivalent feelings about us ending our work together. He was pleased to be in a place where he felt confident to leave, but at the same time knew he was going to miss me. Ending our work together brought back memories of leaving home for Kevin, but this time he felt more prepared.

8

MICHELLE' STORY

> Pretending is an art that is second nature to me,
> But don't be fooled,
> For God's sake don't be fooled.
> I give the impression that I'm secure,
> That all is sunny and unruffled with me, within as well
> As without,
> That confidence is my name and coolness my game,
> The water's calm and I'm in command
> And that I need no one,
> But don't believe me.
> ~Charles C. Finn

My initial contact with Michelle was via a phone call from her. She had self-referred to an addiction specific counsellor who had given Michelle my number because the counsellor had developed a long-term illness and so could not see her.

Michelle told me that she had been dry for three weeks and that she wanted to look at some of the underlying motives for her drinking. I noted that she saw alcohol, or maybe some other addiction, as at least part of the reason why she was seeking counselling. I mentally plotted her on the Cycle of Change. Superficially she seemed to be at the maintenance stage. She said that she had stopped drinking at this point because of concerns around her physical health. This made me wonder if, although physically she was at the maintenance stage whether she was actually at he in contemplation stage psychologically.

Michelle, aged thirty-nine, had been drinking since she was sixteen. She commented that when she went out she was often the last person to leave the pub and that she also found it difficult to curb her drinking. Michelle reported that three weeks previously she had cut down from about two bottles of wine and several spirits a night to nothing. Stopping in this manner can be very dangerous because of the risk of seizures but when asked how she had been after stopping so abruptly, she denied any physical or psychological withdrawal symptoms. I felt shock and confusion about this account as it did not tie in with more usual accounts of alcohol withdrawal.

In our first session I asked how Michelle had felt about her contact with the original counsellor, but Michelle dismissed the idea that she might have had any feelings around it. I noted the conscious lack of affect, or the difficulty in acknowledging it. I wondered whether a disconnection from her emotions had helped her to cope emotionally in the past.

Michelle's face was very youthful. This presentation together with her drinking habit prompted me to think about developmental arrest and the possibility that a dependency transference could develop. She was a large, tall, affable woman with a big smile and a soft, gentle voice. She told me that she thought that she suffered from depression, but that she had not addressed it as she did not want evidence of depression on her medical record. I felt a surge of frustration for the depressed part of her, which was not being allowed public acknowledgement. I wondered whether she also felt frustration at having to hide this part of her.

She frequently used a gentle ripple of laughter when she made fun of her own behaviour and her difficulties or disappointments in life. I noted the absence of the other polarities: sadness, shame and anger.

She was very conscious of her body's restlessness. She rarely sat still, but twitched constantly and jerked her head. She slouched in the chair so she appeared smaller. I wondered about the part of her that did not want to be seen. Her body posture together with her account of the drinking opened my mind to the possible presence of shame.

Her narrative included being in constant physical pain which she believed was due to prescribed medication which she had taken ten years previously and which had now been withdrawn from use by the manufacturer. She complained that the side effects of the drug had caused tingling and numbness in her hands and feet, stomach and chest pains, panic attacks and severe cramps. I noted that these symptoms could also have been caused by excessive drinking.

She wanted the therapy "to keep" her "on course" and to look at some of the underlying issues around why she drank. When she said "on course", I had a vivid image of a huge ship being steered by myself. It felt as though the responsibility for staying on course was being passed over to me. Yet I also noted that she had gone through the detoxification on her own and had only sought help afterwards. I wondered about issues involving trust and dependence.

The denial of negative affect made more sense when Michelle described herself as the "goody two-shoes" of the family. Her younger sister has been seen as the "naughty one" - becoming pregnant at fifteen and going to live in a council house with a much older man. For a short time, her parents refused to have anything to do with the sister. Michelle told me that her father was a master baker and a perfectionist, but it was interesting that she did not mention her mother. When I asked about her mother she told me that she had enjoyed "a very happy childhood". As she said this she indicated the shape of an umbrella with her hand and said that it was "an umbrella type of memory" – one with no detail. She remembered it as "a perfect childhood". She also commented that she had no memory of her childhood before the age of eleven. I noted the possible idealization of her early years given that she could remember no specific events.

When asked about any significant landmarks in her life, Michelle only chose only those events which had occurred recently within her married lifetime. Michelle had been in a stable relationship for ten years. She had left school after A-levels and found a job near home as she felt that her parents could not cope with her going away at that time. She now regretted this. She expressed the difficulty of getting what she wanted out of life because of her fear of disapproval. She had never lived alone and was unsure whether she could manage on her own. Michelle confided that she had always had a partner, and that her romantic relationships always overlapped. She had not spent even a single day "on her own". I noted Michelle's high level of dependence on others and how she had managed her life to accommodate this need.

One of the incidents in her life that Michelle thought of as crucially important to her was having been made redundant from her last job in sales role where she had been very highly paid. She worked very long hours, travelled extensively and spent many evenings "propping up the hotel bar". After the

Addiction - This being human

redundancy Michelle had remained unemployed for eighteen months. She had since set up her own company but it did not keep her occupied much of the time.

Michelle had had no previous experience of counselling/psychotherapy and she had low expectations about what it could provide. She recognised that it could not provide an immediate fix. In fact she told me that she was "very sceptical" about counselling/psychotherapy being able to help at all, but a friend had advised it. I wondered about whether she had engaged partly to please this friend. However, her motivation to stay dry, at this point, seemed high. She told me that eventually she hoped to be able to drink in moderation.

Michelle and I agreed to work together for twelve sessions and to review this contract on the eighth session. I felt that this would be long enough for her to start to understand some of her underlying issues and would allow time for us to explore her triggers and cues for drinking. As she seemed unsure about the efficacy of counselling/ psychotherapy, I thought that this would provide her with enough time to see whether it suited her, or not.

Since Michelle had reported no side effects from alcohol withdrawal, on the surface it appeared that her dependence was psychological, rather than physical. I decided to keep an open mind about this conclusion though because Michelle seemed to be out of touch with her bodily sensations. Also I remembered that she had not wanted the doctor to know about her alcohol intake and I wondered if she was minimising so that I would not know and so she could stay in denial about a possible addictive habit.

A recurring theme was Michelle's general physical condition which was very poor. Her eating, exercise, work, recreation and sleep patterns were all erratic. She reported the existence of a stomach ulcer, cysts on the eyelids and in her nasal passages. She also reported shooting pains and aches in almost every part of her body. She returned often to the account of her hands, arms, feet and the bottoms of her legs being numb. Michelle also liked to remind me that she and others were involved in litigation against the drug manufacturers, but that no case was yet proven against them or the drug. This factor enabled Michelle to stay in denial about the consequences of her drinking. This made it impossible for either of us even to question whether any of the symptoms might be the result of excessive alcohol.

Michelle's job had been very stressful. She carried a high workload and had to work away from home frequently. The job also entailed public speaking, which Michelle had found increasingly difficult. She had started to experience panic attacks just before she was made redundant. Partly the redundancy had come as a relief, but it also left her feeling inadequate. As well the loss of her job had brought financial difficulties to the family since Michelle was the main bread winner.

Michelle and I looked at how alcohol had served her in the past and what the benefits were currently. I hoped that Michelle would be able to link her drinking to specific incidents, thoughts or feelings to help her to begin to create a sense of order out of her chaotic experience of drinking.

Over a period of time it became apparent that Michelle used alcohol for several purposes; to block out physical and emotional pain, to calm herself down and to give her self-confidence, to fill a gap when she was bored, to help her to sleep, to satisfy the "teenage rebellious" aspect of herself and to give her a sense of belonging, for example, when she went out drinking with "the girls".

Addiction - This being human

In order to help Michelle find other substitutes for the alcohol, we looked at alternative ways to gain these benefits, for example, Michelle considered returning to playing the piano to alleviate boredom.

Even at the beginning of our work, we discovered a small part of Michelle that wanted to give up alcohol completely, although most of her still wanted to be able to drink socially. We explored her ambivalence to alcohol. This was aimed at leading Michelle away from her all-or-nothing pattern of thinking, and towards her understanding the different aspects of herself. On the negative side she acknowledged the financial costs of drink and acknowledged the possibility of detrimental effects on her physical well-being. On the positive side, it helped her to deaden life's pains, the focus of all her social life involved drinking alcohol and it seemed to be one of the few pleasures in her life. She explained how she took lots of trouble to organise her everyday life around the access to alcohol. She would volunteer to take her children to the park to play because she passed an off-license on the way. There was, however, an acknowledgement that the anticipation of the first glass gave her a greater buzz than the actual drinking of it did. At this stage, the connection she made between her alcohol consumption and her physical pain was minimised, she saw the majority of the pain as the persistent side-effects of the previously prescribed drug.

Initially I found Michelle absolutely fascinating. I looked forward eagerly to my sessions with her. That fascination probably helped the early working alliance to develop because I hung on her every word - something to which she was not accustomed. I heard a narrative that included extreme behaviour when she was intoxicated including high levels of risk-taking. It reflected a Dr Jekyll and Mr. Hyde lifestyle. At home and at work she was playing and had played "the happily married woman", and yet three evenings a week she spent in the local pub playing "the fastest drinker" and "one of the girls". Frequently she would have a period of binge drinking which left her unconscious. She recounted several episodes of high risk behaviour including an incident where she had come round on a platform of a railway station in a strange town not knowing how she had got there. She explained this behaviour as providing a release because she generally felt "restricted between tight tramlines". I wondered whether the fascination was a tool that Michelle used in relating to others, whether it was a front that she put on to hide the part of her that felt impotent or insignificant.

What initially struck me about Michelle, I understood in terms of Klein's (1946) idea of the 'bad, shameful' parts being split off. Michelle appeared to find life, within the confines of this "straight-jacketed, good self", frustrating. As a reaction to this, she seemed to live out her shadow side with 'the girls' in the pub. I wondered whether this 'bad' self allowed her to act out her anger and other negative emotions in a way that protected both her parents and her partner. Much later on in the sessions, she explained that her mother often made her angry, but she felt unable to say anything to her about the various incidents that provoked that anger. Instead she did not return her mother's phone calls. I understood this as Michelle acting out her anger, rather than being conscious of the anger. In other words she was expressing her anger using passive-aggressive behaviour.

Likewise, I also understood one part of Michelle's self as being dominated by a very demanding Parent. In order to increase Michelle's self awareness and to help her make some sense out of the random chaos she was experiencing, I brought my thinking about the different parts of self to Michelle's attention by using the Adult/ Parent/ Child model. Michelle drew a model of herself using these concepts in which the Parent and

Addiction - This being human

the Child were the main components. She noted that most of her Parent ego state was critical and that a large proportion of her Child ego state had adapted itself to those internalised criticisms.

I pointed out the frequency with which she used the words "should, must, need, ought". We explored what she would 'like' or 'want' to do. She became conscious of the origins of these internalized voices as we made links with how she had experienced her mother, both consciously and unconsciously, as a child. She also came to see that it was these inner voices, rather than some outside figure, that were constraining her within the tram-lines. This came as quite a shock to Michelle, because she had experienced the restriction as something that was being done to her, rather than something she was doing to herself.

It became evident that Michelle experienced the alcohol, quite literally, as bringing a release from the tramlines, rather than herself who had a choice about consuming the alcohol. We looked at the three positions of victim, rescuer and persecutor on the Drama Triangle so that Michelle could begin to question both the dynamic operating between herself and the alcohol and also the similarity in some of her other relationships. I asked her to consider where she would position herself in relation to the alcohol. She immediately put herself in the victim position with alcohol in the rescuer position. After some thought she commented that she thought that the alcohol alternated between rescuer and persecutor. When we explored whether she had any other similar relationships, she mentioned a woman who had enabled her to be accepted by the group of "girls" with whom she drank. Michelle had lent a large sum of money to her and she was now refusing to pay it back. We explored whether her parents, or I, could fit on to the triangle and where we would be located. Michelle saw herself as the rescuer with her parents being the victims. When we looked at our relationship, Michelle saw me as the rescuer and she was again the victim. We talked about this in terms of giving up her power and denying others theirs.

When we came to renew the contract, my initial thoughts about dependency were reinforced as Michelle told me she wanted to continue the therapy as soon as she walked in the door. She commented how wonderful the sessions were and how she was so pleased she had found the "perfect" therapist. I noted that I was probably being experienced as her mother in the transference who was also reported as being "perfect". Winnicott (1958) identifies disillusionment of the idealised mother as one of the functions of the good-enough mothering, and an essential stage of our psychological development. I wondered if this stage of development had been missed and I wondered too if Michelle's perception of an idealized mother had kept her tied to her mother. I considered whether at an unconscious level the idealized mother was experienced as more able to protect her than her own inadequate or damaged grown-up self, given all the good parts of herself that she had invested, or lost in the projection.

Stean (1985), referring to clients who manifest a dependent-transference, comments that these clients are:

> "(F)rightened to be autonomous and separate, usually experiencing maturity as an intensely hostile act. They are so worried about who they have hurt or destroyed that they need constant reassurance that they are still loved and accepted". (p.102)

This seemed to fit with Michelle, but in the initial assessment she had also described her mother as "fragile" and just how this aspect of the mother fitted into the ideal puzzled me. I also

Addiction - This being human

had a body sense that there was an error in my thinking – my experience of Michelle did not quite add up because at one level she seemed to find it difficult to accept help, preferring to be independent. I remained open-minded.

Gradually I came to understand this apparent paradox by holding in mind her unconscious need to be "good" for the parents who were perceived as too fragile to cope with or maintain contact with her wayward sister and Michelle's fear that if she should behave "badly" they would abandon her too. It was as if Michelle acted in a way that would allow her to maintain the image of her mother as "perfect" even though it meant abandoning her own wishes.

As the work continued a recurring theme emerged through Michelle's narrative - a desperate need to impress, please and be liked, be it as Dr Jekyll, by her colleagues and parents, or as Mr. Hyde, by "the girls". These two qualities were often adhered to at great cost, for instance in lending her female drinking colleague £25,000 at a time when she was short of money. During her period of abstinence, she was driving her drinking pals around the country, often at times that were inconvenient to her. With me Michelle always arrived exactly on time and she tended to swallow my words without much thought. Once when she left without paying me, I found several distressed messages on my answerphone.

Within the first few sessions, while we were exploring her critical internalized voices, Michelle suddenly seemed to change her behaviour. She reported that she had become more assertive, rather than flipping between passive and aggressive behaviour. She attempted to talk more intimately with her husband and she tried to sort out several unresolved difficulties in her life. I experienced the suddenness of the change as a shock in the counter-transference and it made me curious about what was going on. At one level, it seemed to fit into Michelle's 'all-or-nothing' way of doing things, but at another level, I could not make any sense of such a rapid change in behaviour, other than in terms of a flight into health.

I decided to explore this behaviour with Michelle in order to uncover what I thought might be unconscious processes. I became aware that she had heard criticism in my observations and was trying to change the behaviours of which she thought I disapproved. However as time progressed, she found that these changes could not be sustained as she was merely trying to fit in with her perception of my ideals.

After Michelle's new forced behaviour ceased, it was as if she was at sea. Not knowing, or able to guess at, how I wanted her to 'perform', she went into a period of 'stuckness' and depression. Without the drink Michelle had become more conscious of her problems including several areas of unfinished business. She told me how she had created a romantic setting on a tropical beach to propose to her boyfriend and then disclosed, quite unexpectedly, that she had found him in bed with another woman on the eve of their wedding. She recounted how she had returned home earlier than expected to find him with an old girlfriend. She stated that she gone along with the wedding because of all the effort her parents had put into organising it. As she was telling me my body once again went into shock. Michelle had previously described the marriage as "happy". I wondered how many people's shock I was carrying in the counter-transference and whether some of it might also belong to her boyfriend's shock as he was caught in the act. Given the cost to Michelle, it was an extreme form of people-pleasing. When I asked her how she felt about this, she giggled and said that she sometimes regretted it, but reiterated that she had not wanted to disappoint them and had not felt able to cope with all the inconvenience and disruption

Addiction - This being human

it would have caused for others. Michelle then went on to tell me about the "betrayal" she felt over the unpaid loan by her female drinking companion. She had never even suspected that the money would not be paid back on time. I wondered if the two were related but Michelle could not make a link. She seemed to be in denial about the hurt and betrayal to do with her partner's actions.

Without the alcohol to dull Michelle's emotional life, she sometimes reported feelings of frustration, anger, guilt, embarrassment and shame. Although these feelings were named they did not seem to be experienced in her body and were not communicated or felt in the counter-transference. The only sensation I often picked up were those of shock. I wondered whether shock had been a part of Michelle's early life and whether she was living in a state of shock as a married woman given what had taken place prior to the marriage and the huge loss of her romantic image of the relationship with her husband.

Developmentally I understood Michelle's people-pleasing nature in terms of Winnicott's (1960) concept of the False Self which he sees as a self which develops by "compliance with environmental demands" (p147). He sees the origin of the False Self in the mother/infant relationship in cases where rather than the mother attuning to the infant's needs, the infant accepts, or falls in line with the mother's needs/wishes. This can be seen as a creative adjustment; a way in which we adjust our behaviour to fit into the environment in which we find ourselves. While this keeps us safe in the original environment, usually the family home, because it is an unconscious adjusting usually we do not readjust when the environment changes and so use redundant strategies often to our cost.

I decided to explore her people-pleasing behaviour with her

Ronnie Aaronson

so that she might gain some insight into the unconscious processes involved in it. I linked her people-pleasing behaviour towards her parents, her drinking buddies, and to me with her early learning. I hoped that this would give Michelle a sense of self-history, so that she could see herself as a continuous, developing self. We came to understand how it gave her a sense of belonging and it also brought to Michelle's consciousness her fear of abandonment, which we discovered stopped her from saying "no" when she wanted to. She claimed that placing other peoples' needs before her own boosted her self-esteem.

Later on in the work, I was able to point out the paradox between how Michelle experienced her mother as "infuriating" when she was accommodating with her and Michelle's assumption that when she was accommodating with her colleagues, she was pleasing them. I thought that Michelle would at least be curious about this incongruence, but she was unable to hear or to make any sense of it.

I faced a constant dilemma around assessing Michelle's progress towards her goals. I kept an open mind and considered each small step potentially as a movement forward prompted by the 'true' or 'core' self and at the same time I also wondered about the possibility of a regressive step in terms of her need to please me.

Five months into the work, and exactly six months after Michelle had given up drinking, she started to drink again. This was planned and in line with her initial ideas about becoming a social drinker. The drinking initially brought Michelle feelings of relief at having escaped the tramlines, but it did not lift the depression or the stuckness. At this point we renegotiated our contract since we had accomplished the aims of the initial arrangement I also felt it might influence the stuckness. Michelle wanted us to work on monitoring her

Addiction - This being human

drinking so that it should not become "out of control". She felt that our weekly session brought some order and routine into her life.

Another one of Michelle's recurring themes was a sense of "not being heard". Although her mother went to great lengths to meet her practical needs, at another level she was not being heard. Michelle related how her emotions had "always been swept under the carpet". I thought about her use of alcohol "to calm her down" in terms of the 'container' and 'contained'. It seemed probable that Michelle's mother had been unable to contain her anxieties when she was an infant; Michelle had not been able to internalize this capacity and therefore could not now contain her own anxieties. In the past she had relied on the alcohol and now she was returning to that way of self-soothing.

Although the return to social drinking had been planned from the outset of the therapy we had become conscious during the course of our work of a part of Michelle that wanted to be totally abstinent: maybe the part of her that wanted to be truly independent. Therefore it was no surprise that Michelle seemed to slightly disapprove of her own return to drinking and her depression became heavier. During the dry period she was able to get in touch with the part of herself that wanted to stay abstinent, but she was not able to sustain her dry behaviour. We began to see a link between her inability to sustain her new assertive behaviour earlier in the work, and her inability to remain abstinent after the six months were up. Just as the assertive behaviour had been adopted for my sake, we came to understand that she had given up for six months to satisfy her partner's needs and to prove a point to her colleagues, rather than because she had wanted to be dry. As our work together had progressed I had assumed wrongly that Michelle had moved to contemplation on the Cycle of Change but now I could see that psychologically she had remained in pre-contemplation.

During this period of depression she described herself as frustrated and stuck. She saw herself as adopting a "siege" mentality and being in a "survival mode" where she had brought the shutters down". It brought to mind "the sweeping of things under the carpet" – the way in which she had described her parents' behaviour and so her childhood experience. She was only able to cope with and do the minimum amount of work– just as much as she felt was necessary to get by. She felt unable to trust her partner and was resentful towards him. She felt isolated, powerless, helpless and overwhelmed by problems and felt that she was "waiting to hit a brick wall". I wondered whether the emotions to do with her husband's pre-marital behaviour were catching up with her.

Consciously, in some measure, "waiting to hit a brick wall" was about Michelle's perception that a financial crisis was looming due to her husband spending money indiscriminately. A part of her welcomed the crisis because she saw it as the only way for him to acknowledge "what spending category" they were in since her redundancy. She wanted him to suffer the consequences of his irresponsible spending. Another part of her dreaded the disappointment that her parents and partner would express, how her colleagues would react to her moving to a smaller home, and how she would cope coming to terms with a less financially secure and flamboyant lifestyle.

Meanwhile I wondered whether she was also talking about herself in terms of the drinking. A lot of drinkers seem to need to reach a crisis, commonly called "rock bottom", before they are able to give up totally. Michelle could not relate to that idea. I also wondered about Michelle's physical health and whether in some way she feared death. It did not feel like the

Addiction - This being human

appropriate time to explore that idea though so I just held it in mind.

It took me a while to notice but eventually I started to see a lack of congruence between the stuckness she talked about in the room and what actually was happening outside the room. This was partly because the "stuckness" in her narrative accorded with my body experience which was a heavy sensation of being pinned to the floor. This enabled me to ignore the activity outside of the room even though the details presented themselves in her narrative.

Outside she was more able to resolve problems as they arose, she tackled unfinished business including taking legal action against her drinking colleague for monies owed and won her case. She started a course of computer training, worked towards expanding her own business, made more quality time available to be with her partner on their own, became tidier and gave herself permission to rest occasionally. The change in Michelle's behaviour was different from the first change and the rate of progress, which was much slower and felt more integrated and sustainable.

Once I became aware of the inconsistency between the stuckness in and outside of the room, we were able identify that the stuckness she felt reflected her motivation level, rather than the lack of activity. Although she was taking action it was undertaken with resentment and minimal enthusiasm. She commented that even though she had won her legal case to regain the £25,000 loan, a part of her was depressed because it would now take longer to reach a financial crisis point and for her husband to rein in his spending. She was looking forward to his "downfall". Again we were able to identify that the behaviour outside the room was what she felt she should do, rather than what she wanted to do. So what had seemed like new behaviours were actually old behaviour patterns disguised.

Gradually we also came to understand part of the stuckness as a manifestation of her ambivalence. One part of the self "needed" to and "wanted" to get back to work and refused to give up the image of herself as a "high-flyer", while another part was terrified of returning to the experience of panic attacks and other stresses that employment had come to represent and instead wanted to escape the responsibilities it entailed.

As Michelle's business was dwindling and failing to keep her occupied, despite her renewed efforts, she decided to take on some voluntary work. She thought that if her time was more occupied, she would be less bored. She would also need to be sober several hours before working and so it was more likely that she could remain dry. It seemed that now she was switching her responsibility for staying sober onto work, in much the same way that she gave responsibility for being intoxicated to alcohol - rather than her action of choosing to drink alcohol. When I pointed this out, she could not, or did not want to, hear it. I noted that 'not hearing' was becoming a theme in the room for us. I thought again about the strength of denial and the enormity of the pain that it was holding at bay.

Exploring Michelle's depression we came to see it, at least in part, as her going through a mourning process. She was coming to terms with the life that she was in, rather than the "romantic" wish that she once had for her life: coming to terms with the loss of her ability to be a financial "high-flyer".

The weight of the depression and its stuckness aroused feelings of despair and frustration in me too as we sat through it together. Now instead of being fascinated and looking forward to our sessions, I felt a dread as our sessions approached. I

Addiction - This being human

thought about these feelings as representing the two different life experiences: the excitement of outside the "tramlines" and the dread of the experience between them. I wondered if Michelle was dreading coming to the sessions as well. We sat for what seemed liked hours and hours with depression and heaviness. Her own response to the depression was initially governed by her critical voice, which told her to stop making such a fuss and to "get on with it." My own feelings prompted two fantasies of how to respond. The first was to ignore the depression, dismiss her feelings and save myself the discomfort, which I could relate to her mother's reaction to her emotions. The second was an urge to shake the feelings out of Michelle.

My fantasies brought to mind the work of Ogden (1997). He has drawn attention to the connectedness between the therapist's fantasies and the client. Michelle had told me previously that her mother had "swept all her emotional problems" under the carpet, I now wondered whether someone else had also tried to shake them out of her as well.

This seemed to fit with the physical sensations I had experienced in my work with Michelle. Several times I had experienced a severe shock reaction. For example, I felt a blow to my body when Michelle reported that she had cut down from two bottles of wine and several spirits a night to nothing. I experienced a similar blow to my body together with a sense of disorientation at what appeared to be her sudden change in behaviour and again when she had related the sexual betrayal. Each time as the shock happened, I lost my ability to think or act. This brought the Drama Triangle into my consciousness again. There was lots of evidence that Michelle was often in the victim state of mind.

Up to this point in our work, I had only felt I made real contact with Michelle on very few occasions. One of these occurred when she commented that truly she did not enjoy drinking with the girls and "getting smashed", but that her need to belong was a large part of her motivation for those activities. It was only on rare occasions that I glimpsed the hurt, vulnerable Michelle.

During the stuck weeks, I decided that Michelle and I should look more closely at her relationship with her parents and their relationship with each other. I hoped to provide Michelle with a sense of continuity. Initially, Michelle described her parents primarily in two contradictory ways. First, as the parents who had met all her needs: the parents who had been perfect. Secondly, as parents that were too fragile to cope with the demands of everyday life. I pointed to the inconsistency and a clearer picture emerged – parents who had managed her physical, but not her emotional needs.

Looking at the family dynamics brought to the foreground not only how frequently Michelle had had contact with her parents but also the lack of any real intimacy. Michelle explained how her father and she often spent time together, but always doing something practical, such as making shelves or surfing the internet. The only time Michelle became tearful was commenting that her father had never told her he loved her.

Gradually she was able to voice that at times she found her mother "infuriating". Her mother never said "no" and made huge self-sacrifices to fall in with Michelle's requests. Considering the invisibility of her mother due to the mother's lack of boundaries, and the absence of my emotions in the counter-transference with Michelle, I began to think about Michelle and her mother in terms of confluence. MacKewn (1997) describes confluence as what happens when "two people, or two parts of the field, flow together with no sense of differentiation" (p27). Focusing on the family dynamics,

Addiction - This being human

provided clues which enabled me to think in more depth about my relationship with Michelle. I was able to consider this confluent 'prototype' being re-enacted between Michelle and myself. It explained why we rarely had true emotional contact. Clarkson (1999) comments how confluence hinders real contact.

I remembered how my initial feelings of fascination for Michelle's narrative had been compelling in the first few sessions and noted that it had been the narrative which had hooked me, rather than the emotions underlying. I started to understand how I had been pulled into playing the "prototype" script outside my awareness. I had repeated the role of the mother who never heard Michelle's pain.

I also considered Michelle's part in this dynamic. Attuning to Michelle was made difficult by her use of language: everything was gravely understated. Talking about the occasion when she almost got knifed, she described her feelings as "flat". And she presented with a flat affect. Her emotions seemed only very rarely to engage with what was happening to her. She talked at great speed with few pauses and any emergent emotions were passed over quickly. This rarely gave enough time for my emotions to surface in the counter-transference. I could see how her tendency to dissociate from her feelings and the lack of any real contact had served her in the past to make herself acceptable to her parents. These creative adjustments, however, made it impossible for her to make an impact, to get through to others, and indeed perhaps to contact herself in the present. I brought these processes to her attention.

These revelations helped me to realise that I would need to act as an amplifier for Michelle's feelings by paraphrasing her narrative in a manner that would incorporate the appropriate feelings. When she described an event, I had to make a conscious effort to stand back, hear the narrative, watch the scene, get in touch with my feelings and then relay them to her. Our therapeutic relationship reached a different level once I started to engage in this way with the hidden, cut-off emotions camouflaged by the words and to reflect them back to her.

Michelle was rarely certain how she felt about things. She frequently relied on others to make both trivial and important decisions. When I asked her how she felt, she often responded with "I think……". The head/body split was in evidence. In Michelle's family expressed emotions, especially those which were negative, were "swept under the carpet". They were not valued. Consequently Michelle had learnt never to express them. Self-disclosure about how I was feeling became an important part of our work together. I named and shared my emotions with Michelle about how I was affected by her narrative. I watched her physical body movements and brought them to her attention. My disclosures helped her to name emotions and gave her permission to express her own. She became gradually clearer about what emotions were behind certain physical signals.

Michelle's lack of affect can be linked to the concept of shame. Fraiberg (1982) describes how sadness, fear and anger can be transformed into the shaming process. She sees this as a defence by infants against the potential rupture in relationship with the adult for whom these affects are not acceptable. Michelle could identify with this idea. She also felt embarrassed about her body, her acting out and her thoughts. The understanding of shame as fundamental to the development of the psyche, along with its potential to remain hidden and untouched by the therapeutic relationship influenced my consideration around the pace of work with Michelle.

Erskine (1995) comments that to "define or confront someone,

Addiction - This being human

even if accurately, may devalue and humiliate them" (p106). To lessen Michelle's sense of shame I tried to respond to her with empathy and attunement in a non-judgmental way. By remaining consistently non-judgmental yet compassionate towards the 'bad' part of the client, I aimed to provide a less critical internal voice. In time I hoped that this might enable her to incorporate more of her 'bad' self into her core sense of self.

While Michelle was still drinking regularly and about eight months into the work we had an interesting session. Michelle's parents would often phone her up and start a conversation by asking "Do you want a good laugh…?" before going on to tell her about something terrible that had happened to them. These incidents filled Michelle with despair. Now Michelle was laughing at how she had created her own company as a façade. She described it as a play in which she was the director. She could look respectable to her partner, parents or others and hold onto her dignity, but it created lots of unstructured time in which she could drink and be idle. I pointed out how she was laughing at a great tragedy in which she was the main character, in the same way that her parents twisted disasters into humour. I also wondered whether she was attending our sessions as a façade. By attending she could claim she was doing something constructive about her problem to the outside world. I wondered however if in practice the sessions only served as an aid to her self-deception.

As the impact of this tragedy hit me, I decided to reveal the impact of her words on my body in order to get her in touch, albeit remotely, with her affective-self. It caused a pain in my chest and took my breath away. I felt overwhelmed with sadness. I also commented how it could be seen as funny if it weren't for the fact that she was killing herself. This comment was intended to shock and it did. We looked at which part of her was pleased with the façade and which part of her it was serving. Michelle came to the conclusion that she was unconsciously "getting one over" on her parents and husband. Michelle acknowledged that her resentment lay behind her actions, and when I amplified this to "anger", she agreed. A part of me wanted to amplify the feeling to 'rage' but I decided against it. It felt that Michelle had taken a large enough step in reclaiming her anger.

After that session the stuckness dissipated. It was as if the shock had been her "brick wall". Michelle started to reveal more about her emotional self. She stopped talking only about practicalities and began to talk also about her feelings, including her hurt and her pain in her relationships with her mother and partner. She talked to her partner about how she felt. She became more in touch with her anger and resentment generally. She was able to express these emotions in words and I could pick up their embodiment in the counter-transference. Michelle's shame concerning expressing emotions was diminishing. This session saw her move further into contemplation.

Michelle slid back relatively quickly to her original pattern of drinking something most afternoons and evenings as well as drinking heavily three nights of the week; she was also coming to terms with the fact that she could not be a social drinker. Once again we renegotiated the contract because Michelle said she "needed" to work towards abstinence, we made that our goal. She was now at the action stage on the Cycle of Change.

We began to discuss how she often went outside her "tramlines" to make an impact, rather than being able to integrate her ability to make an impact on another person into her everyday life, for example her drinking with the girls often resulted in "yobbish" behaviour. Her impactful part of self appeared to be split-off. I wondered about her unconscious fantasies to harm others. In particular I wondered whether splitting-off her impactful self served an unconscious fear of damaging her parents. Melanie Klein's (1952) notion of 'reparation' seemed to fit with Michelle paying for her parents to have several very expensive cruises.

While we were being curious about her family dynamics, Michelle became conscious of the guilt that her parents projected onto her. This reminded me that Cashdan (1988) comments on a form of projective identification which structures relationships "so that the major emotional component is that of self-sacrifice" (p74). For example, Michelle's parents told her how long and how much they had saved to take her to the pantomime and then how they all had to leave because Michelle had cried inconsolably at one of the characters.

I then started to have feelings of guilt about my fee, as Michelle mentioned financial difficulties. It made me wonder whether paying me every week, while she was financially insecure, was an unconscious acting out of this dynamic. She could not connect with the suggestion, but at the beginning of the following session she commented that she had noticed that she repeated this dynamic, the projection of guilt, with most of her social contacts. For example, Michelle was asked to drive a friend to the airport at a time when she had been expected at the volunteer centre, but she agreed nevertheless. Afterwards, as her resentment grew towards this friend, she made sarcastic comments about the incident, promoting guilt in the friend.

Her lack of emotional affect, her need to please others and her perceived inability to initiate any new behaviour made me question Michelle's sense of self. Michelle's lack of self-agency has been symbolized by her understanding that she had to wait "to see what turns up" or wait "to hit a brick wall" before she could act. It was as though she only felt able to respond to someone, or something, if events were going badly, rather than initiating action. She described herself as an object travelling along a conveyor belt being processed by people and events as she passed by. In order to promote a sense of self-agency, I encouraged the substance of narrative in every day events, so that her actions became attached to the consequences of the action. I celebrated all occasions when she did take the initiative, or accomplished something, for example, when she found out the process necessary to apply for her voluntary work.

We looked at Michelle's early learning; how she had adjusted to the environment in which she found herself and how this affected her in the present. We looked by what means her drinking could be understood as a way to contain her anxieties and I pointed out how at the beginning, before she became addicted to the substance, this would have been effective. Similarly, when Michelle spoke of her stupidity at organizing her life around drinking possibilities, I pointed out that when she wanted to drink this could be seen as creative and how, only now that she wanted to stay dry, did it seem silly. Also, I pointed out that if she had been that inventive in order to get hold of alcohol, she could be equally creative now to stay dry. Michelle experienced shame about her drinking habit, especially when she had been "on a bender". I pointed out that this was how she had learnt to deal with her difficult emotions.

Michelle only had a dim sense of herself as a continuous being through time. Although her recent sense of self-history was more vivid, Michelle had no memories that extended back before eleven years of age. I have wondered about this in terms of attachment theory. Main (1994) found a correlation between being unable to produce a cohesive narrative about a childhood and insecure attachment. Michelle's recollection of her recent history has probably not been helped by her heavy drinking which not only allows an individual to live life in a blur, but also causes physiological damage to the brain which affects short term memory. I made links between Michelle's current experience and her remembered experiences wherever possible in order to give her a sense of continuity.

Michelle's sense of self-cohesion seemed poor too. She appeared to be cut off, to a large extent, from her bodily sensations. Michelle's words that she was waiting to hit a brick wall had a huge impact on my own body. It was as if I was bracing my body for the collision. Her lack of sensation helped to confirm my thinking about her disconnection from her bodily sensations. I brought my own body sensations to Michelle's notice. She understood them as being related to the pains in her body, but she still held onto the idea that most of her pain was due to the after-effects of the previously prescribed medication.

After Michelle had been in contemplation for several months, she started one of our sessions by commenting how she experienced me as "totally disinterested" in what she had been saying during our previous session. I found this curious because that had not been my experience: nothing had felt different to me and. I asked her to say more about it and she mimed someone examining and cleaning their fingernails, and then someone tapping their fingernails on the arm of the chair. I asked whether she remembered me doing either of those in the session. She thought for a long time and then she replied that she actually thought it was her that was bored with hearing the same old excuses over and over and that she had projected that on to me. We noted the impact that the projection could have made on our relationship, had she not owned it, and wondered how similar projections might have affected other relationships.

About four weeks after this session Michelle commented that now she could accept that she was unable to give up drinking by herself. What emerged from that discussion was that for about three months previously Michelle had planned each week to give up drinking on the Sunday. However, while attempting to have her last drink each Friday she had over-indulged so she then needed alcohol on the Sunday to survive the withdrawal effects. I was shocked at the fact that she had not mentioned this in any of our previous sessions. I noticed again her tendency to go it alone without the support that was being offered.

This disclosure seemed to trigger a change in my thinking and ultimately in Michelle's behaviour. We had talked before about Michelle's inability to trust, and therefore her inability to rely on anyone else. Here was a powerful example of just that. Our contract at this stage was to achieve abstinence. Yet here was Michelle trying to achieve it alone and not even mentioning it in the sessions.

This also changed my thinking about Michelle in terms of dependency. Previously I had been rather confused because I was receiving ambivalent visual, auditory and body-felt messages about this. The material conflicted. In some ways Michelle seemed strongly dependent and yet there was also a tendency to achieve everything on her own. Now I could see Michelle more in terms of someone who was dependent, but who was actually in denial about it because of the terror that "being dependent" on another person evoked. I understood her independence now as a psuedo-independence. She seemed to be living up to a projected role of an independent person, rather than being one.

Addiction - This being human

I now saw her relationship with alcohol more in terms of her dependency needs being acted out with an object that she thought she could trust. I wondered whether her current relationship with her parents, with whom she had almost daily contact, was her way of trying to work through her dependency needs with them because she had been unable to depend on them as a child. I got a different sense of the fixed pattern around her binge drinking and wondered whether it too could be understood in terms of wanting to surrender control to, or be dependent on, another, albeit an object as a hope that this time, it might be different and that she would not be let down. I felt that gradually she was starting to trust me. However, I could imagine on the one hand her feelings of terror at the thought of being dependent on me, and on the other hand the driving force of her relational, dependency need. The recognition of this sense of ambivalence brought more clarity for us about the former stuckness. This change in thinking affected the way I was with Michelle in the room – I felt more compassionate towards her. The shift in me had an impact on our relationship and I felt clearly that the contact between us deepened.

From this point onwards Michelle rarely used language to camouflage her serious physical or emotional difficulties. Laughter was reserved for the trivial upsets in life. I could see too that her denial around her drinking and her body and emotional pain and the relationship between the two was at last being acknowledged. Commenting on the difference of contact between us, Michelle commented that now she "just spoke to me". She clarified this by saying that at the beginning of our work together she had heard what I said, had quickly guessed which reply I wanted, and then replied to me. She noticed that her "internal auditor" had vanished and said how much more relaxing that was. I could see that the Parent ego state had loosened its grip on at least her interactions with me at least.

While Michelle was in the action phase of the Cycle of Change, I wondered whether getting her more in touch with sensation might help. We thus spent a few sessions focusing solely on Michelle's body sensations. After those sessions Michelle reported that her body had become so painful that she had spent a whole day in bed. This was a first for Michelle as usually her critical Parent would not allow her to take time off work.

She had stopped working because her right hand had gone into spasm – a cramp, which held her hand in a hook. She could not move it. We explored her body's reaction to being heard in the previous sessions. She talked about her body "having given up hope that it would be heard" and that how now that she was listening, she could hear it screaming at her. Exploring what the right hand might be trying to say, Michelle linked it to work and her fear of returning to employment. I was interested that she did not mention lifting glasses of wine, but did not offer this interpretation in case she thought I was being critical of her drinking and gave up again – this time in order to please me.

After that session we then had our Christmas break. When Michelle returned she began our session by relating how over the break her computer had crashed, leaving her with no means of working and plenty of time on her hands. With the loss of the structure to her day, she drank excessively to a point that had shocked even her. She commented that she had "hit her brick wall". She concluded this catalogue of disasters by telling me that she had been dry for one week. She was reluctant to accept my praise for one week's abstinence and seemed down. I questioned whether our two missed sessions over the break had made any impact on her and for the first time she acknowledged that perhaps they had.

Over the next few sessions Michelle, having rejected my suggestion on several occasions that AA might help, suggested that she would like to talk about the possibility of attending. Exploring this option uncovered her ambivalence towards the suggestion. She wondered what sort of people went to AA. She noted her dislike of groups in general but then she acknowledged that she needed support. I saw this as a giant step for Michelle. She had also come to a conclusion that she had been using the prescribed medication as an excuse, and admitted that she now believed that most of her body was being affected badly by the alcohol. She further commented that the last time she had given up alcohol she had not felt much better because she had replaced the wine with an energy drink. This was another detail that she had held back from me up until this point.

After about nineteen months since we began our work, Michelle left counselling. She had been dry for seven months. She had lost three stone in weight. She had also taken on the responsibility for all the cooking at home, which kept her occupied at her most vulnerable time of day. In addition she had begun to attend a self-help group as well as AA, was looking after herself and was optimistic about the future.

9

THIS BEING HUMAN

> Every human being is a work in progress
> that is slowly but inexorably moving towards
> perfection. We are each an unfinished work of
> art both waiting and striving to be completed.
> …….. because humanity is a fine art of skilled
> penmanship where every single dot is equally
> important for the entire picture.
> ~Elif Shafak

Within the context of the self-harm continuum, addictive behaviour becomes normalised. It then follows that counselling and psychotherapy are as appropriate for individuals seeking help with their excessive substance use as any other human being struggling to cope with their emotional difficulties. The only difference is that they often need more help in order to withdraw from their habit because of the nature of an addictive substance. Counsellors and psychotherapists specialising in addiction understand the need to prepare the ground before the deeper work of counselling or psychotherapy can take place.

Wanigaratne and Keaney (2002) have argued that treatment should provide:

integrative stepped-care approach. The approaches should follow a sequence which parallels the recovery process and includes behavioural approaches, cognitive-behavioural, relapse prevention techniques alongside counselling and finally psychotherapy." (p123)

They propose the following treatment steps:

1. Behavioural approaches when heavy drug or alcohol use is creating chaos or problems

2. Motivational interviewing techniques as the drug use comes under control and stability is achieved

3. Relapse prevention and counselling when drinking or drug taking has reduced substantially and finally when abstinence has been achieved

4. Psychotherapy/ counselling to deal with the underlying issues

It makes sense that counselling, when used to help with problem substance use, requires a stepped approach because where a person sits on the Cycle of Change influences where they are psychologically, emotionally and physically and this points to which strategies are likely to be most helpful.

Counselling, when referred to in the field of addiction, is a term which covers many ways of being and many different techniques: just listening and reflecting back, motivational interviewing strategies, setting cognitive behavioural exercises, helping to identify triggers, suggesting and exploring individual strategies for cutting back, working on relapse prevention strategies, teaching individuals how to ground themselves,

Addiction - This being human

normalising emotional states, linking past events to present behaviours, bringing the unconscious into awareness through interpretation and working through deeper issues. Each form has its time, place and function on the journey of recovery. For the emotional development of individuals seeking treatment what is important is for them to be met where they are. For instance, it would be nonsensical to make an elaborate interpretation at a point when the individual seeking help is still using or drinking.

If we do not meet individuals where they are, our approach will be inaccessible to those we are trying to help. When people first come for help they usually need to talk, to get whatever they are struggling with emotionally off their chest. They are often anxious about starting treatment and meeting a new counsellor and so they might need to talk a lot, to be on transmit. They need to be listened to without too many interventions. They need to have their feelings made sense of, validated and normalised. Individuals who are still using a substance might need support either to withdraw slowly or to prepare psychologically for a chemical detoxification. If individuals reduce their alcohol intake themselves, rather than relying on a form of medication like Librium, they take back their sense of power, rather than relying on yet another drug; they begin to get a sense of self-agency.

When working to support those using a substance we need to work towards reducing stress and anxiety levels. Once an individual's fear system is operating less of the time, they will be more able to respond in a more logical manner, rather than react from an unconscious habit. Boundaries around the therapeutic setting and our actions can all help to provide a safe space in which anxiety can be talked through and reduced.

There comes a point in treatment when individuals are more

contained. At this stage they are better able to take in and be receptive so they can move on to look at relapse prevention techniques and personal development, in particular looking at self- esteem, relationships, shame and other challenging elements of their lives. A historical context can be helpful in supporting a stronger sense of self. For example, once someone can understand why their self-esteem is so low and how they are perpetuating it by treating themselves in the same way that they were treated by their primary carers, they start to understand why they behave as they do in the present moment. By relating their current behaviour to their past experience, they gain a sense of their historical self; that is their self developing over time. Once unconscious self-destructive thoughts or behaviours are brought into awareness they can be challenged. As individuals start to experiment with changed behaviours in a safe setting, they increased their perception of them self as an evolving entity.

Individuals need to understand why they are using a substance so that they can learn new behaviours to combat or to identify and resist the trigger. For example, if they use when their anxiety levels are overwhelming, they might usefully learn relaxation techniques and learn to identify what makes them stressed, so that they can avoid certain situations

One-to-one counselling can run along side personal development which is being delivered in a group setting. An understanding that overwhelming emotions are generally historical helps to manage the present, by grounding themselves and noticing the reality of what is happening in the here and now, containment can be achieved.

The personal development stage of treatment prompts issues from the past to come into focus. While looking at past relationships many come to realise for the first time that they played the role of the care-taker in their family, even as a small child and that this role is still taken on in the present. By talking these issues through with their therapist they can process the information and integrate it into their developing sense of who they are.

Therapists can help to heal the body/mind split. At the beginning of the counselling process individuals who have lived in their heads preface statements about how they feel with "I think…". This might indicate that they are struggling for vocabulary. It might also show them to be trying to work out how they feel by using their mind, rather than listening to their body. As individuals slowly get more accustomed to checking out their bodily sensations and emotions, the sense of an affective self emerges: a self that is in touch with emotions and knows what is wanted or needed in any particular moment. By being non-judgemental and supporting the individual to be in touch with an increasingly wide range of emotions, split-off parts of self, which hitherto were thought to be unacceptable, can be integrated or re-integrated. Bodywork, as we have seen, can also help enormously in this area.

The initial loss at birth of the security, warmth and comfort which we experienced in the womb, will be a larger loss if our mother is unable to be emotionally present, or attend to our physical needs. It is possible for this profound loss to be emotionally re-ignited as we experience subsequent losses *as if* they were the initial loss. This is the body/mind transferring our past experience to our present experience, just as this transference can happen in relationships, so it also can happen in familiar situations. Many people who use substances have had profound losses or a series of smaller losses.

It is useful to bear in mind that giving up a substance is usually experienced as a big loss in itself: such a big loss that it can trigger the grieving process and bring forth denial, anger, despair and hopefully ultimately acceptance. This is a normal process but it is yet another difficulty in the early months of sobriety. Acknowledging the loss and grief brought about by sobriety can highlight the degree to which alcohol or drugs served as a support in the past. It is important to see ambivalence as a normal and healthy aspect of change. It is useful at this time to look at the disadvantages and also the advantages of using. If practitioners only talk about the negative effects of substance use, clients will probably hold onto the positive aspects of their use more tightly. If we are ambivalent about any aspect of change, as soon as someone advises us to choose one side over the other, we naturally veer towards the other choice. If we are not sure whether or not to move house, once someone recommends we do, we tend to favour staying where we are. In that way, both sides of the ambivalence are naturally represented.

Once we have the repeated experience of someone who is attuned to our emotional state, who can bear our pain and also help us to make sense of and process it, we are much more likely to be able to internalise that relationship. A profound or fundamental need then is the opportunity for people who are dependent on substances to be in a long-term, non-judgemental and therefore non-shaming therapeutic relationship, so that they are able to trust that person and become temporarily dependent on them, instead of the substance. In this way, the counsellor can be internalised as a good-enough other, that is someone who is able to contain their emotions. This will gradually reinforce their blossoming sense of a good-enough sense of self and their own newly learned ability to self-soothe without the use of a substance and they will naturally move into independence.

When Jane's partner failed to arrive at the agreed time, we saw

Addiction - This being human

how Jane ate biscuits to fill the void she felt inside when she could not make sense of or manage her anxiety at being left waiting. She did not have an internalised supporting mother who could soothe that anxiety. Sometimes we drink and/or eat to fill an emotional emptiness: there is an unconscious association between having contact with another human being and feeling full; in our first relationship as we feed and fill our stomachs, we usually have very close physical contact with the one that feeds us.

To speed up the internalisation process it would be useful to allocate and introduce a counsellor at the beginning of the recovery journey, even though at this point the person may be in no place to engage with anything other than being listened to. It can be reassuring for the person starting out on their recovery journey to feel that someone is keeping them in mind, since people using substances have frequently become socially isolated from their peers and cut off from their families. At this stage the therapeutic relationship could provide hope, comfort, and a sense that someone is travelling alongside them. The counsellor and the client could begin to establish the working alliance. This connection could then be maintained until the end of the recovery journey.

Research has shown that success in therapy is much more to do with the relationship between the therapist and client than any other factors (Frank 1979, Hynan 1981, Luborsky et al 1983 and Hill 1989 cited in P. Clarkson, 1995). Rogers (1951) commenting on person-centred therapy, claims:

> "The process of therapy is seen as being synonymous with the experiential relationship between client and therapist. Therapy consists in experiencing the self in a wide range of ways in an emotionally meaningful relationship with the therapist. The words – of either

client or counsellor – are seen as having minimal importance compared with the present emotional relationship which exists between the two." (p172)

To empower an individual who sees himself as a victim and who indeed probably was a victim of abuse or neglect earlier in life, it is important for him to have the experience of making an impact. Working from an equal power base we are more likely to facilitate this experience. By communicating our warmth, unconditional positive regard, our empathy and by our congruence we offer a real and reparative relationship. Without using a blank screen to invite the transference, we just work with it when it arises. In this way we can feed back the impact that the individual has on us and they begin to gain not only a sense of the consequences of their actions but also of their fledgling ability to change their circumstances and the environment: this is the beginning of self-agency. When the relationship develops from equality as human beings, we are also less likely to shame and cajole someone who has become used to being shamed and cajoled. As practitioners, this equality also protects us from being experienced in the transference, no matter what our intention, as the bully or the abuser.

Our own mental health and emotional welfare relies on our capacity to feel sensations, make sense of them and then to communicate them to another, or in some other way to discharge the energy. Once we acknowledge that most people use alcohol or drugs in order to cope with overwhelming feelings, it is easier to work with the individual's goals and aims. If people want to control their drinking, I believe we should support them with that goal, even if we know it is unrealistic. We can tell the individual that their drinking history suggests that it is very unlikely they will be able to control it, but that we will be happy to support them to see if this is true or not. If we are willing to support them where they are, we encourage them to achieve their own goal, we support their independence, their body felt sense of what is right and we do not push them into a state of fear.

By insisting that an individual becomes abstinent when their own goal is otherwise, we push *our* needs onto them. This asks and encourages them to rely on their internalised critical other, which is often the part of themselves that carries out the self-harming activity. If, on the other hand, we support individuals to attain the goals that arise from their core self, whatever those goals might be at the time, we support and enhance their self-care system. Then, as practitioners, our actions are congruent with what we are trying to help people achieve in the long-term; a reduced level of self-harming behaviour and an improved and sustainable level of self-care.

Once individuals are stable and held by the predictability of the service offered and all that happens within it, they start to have the experience of being contained. Focusing on the body, bringing physical and emotional sensations back into awareness and helping individuals to understand their sensations, can help them to integrate the body/mind split. I believe strongly that teaching what emotions are, their function, their essence, their names, their physiological impact and how to deal with them is essential for sustainable recovery.

In one-to-one counselling, empathic responses can soothe, normalise and validate the individual's emotional states. Links can be made between past trauma and current self-harming behaviour, making sense of what may have seemed like random madness. A strong sense of self, of who we are, can be established. By helping individuals to build a personal narrative, they begin to get a sense of their historical self;

they begin to understand the connection between actions and consequences.

Once the foundations have been laid for the individual to tolerate and manage their emotions by continual containment from the therapist and by teaching the individual to ground himself – deeper therapeutic work can be started safely. If this deeper work is attempted before the individual can manage their emotions, it is likely to prompt a lapse, or relapse as they regress to old ways of self-soothing.

Ultimately, what is needed to make life-long abstinence achievable and to make life itself enjoyable, is for the body/mind split to be healed and for split-off parts of the self to be reclaimed. Only then can an integrated and full sense of self be established. Stern (1998) has identified self-agency, self-affectivity, self-history and self-coherence as components that can help to establish a sense of self (p71). Once individuals have a firm sense of self, addictive behaviours, including co-dependency, automatically diminish as they feel more grounded and able to cope. Similarly, behaviours that are taught as part of the rehabilitation process can be assimilated rather than added on as an appendage. For example, how can we be expected to become assertive in order to get our needs met when we are unable to identify our needs? How can our self-esteem flourish if we feel either empty with no real sense of our self, or feel intrinsically bad at the core, as a result of having been persistently abused and/or shamed in childhood?

In the absence of a good-enough long-term relationship, the individual might still carry the burden of a punitive, critical voice in his head together with the lack of an internalised caring voice. This combination is likely to set up repeated incidents of self-shaming as the individual repeats his early learning about how to be. We all feel safe and reassured by what is known.

If an individual has known excessive criticism and sha
since he was a child; shame and criticism will feel familiar and
safe. Similar situations might be sought out and the process
repeated unconsciously. Sadly, this has a devastating physical
and psychological effect when the acting out takes the form
of substance abuse.

It is paramount to attune to each individual client. Recovery
journeys will be as individual as those people setting out on
the recovery path. Initially, some people will find that the
easiest way to become sober is to use the critical, punitive
side of their self: sobriety by will-power alone. However, if
they are left to rely on this part of themselves in the longer-
term, without developing their self-nurturing habits, their
lives will probably feel constrained; an existence, rather than
a fully-engaged, enjoyable and balanced way of life. If their
nurturing side is not encouraged, it is likely that eventually
they will return to their habitual self-harming behaviours.
All long-term sustainable abstinence involves improved self-
care in every area of our lives. This is difficult to maintain if
the internalised critical/punitive voice is not challenged and
diminished. Theories about shame, together with those about
containment and good-enough mothering suggest that long-
term sobriety depends on internalising a voice which is caring,
compassionate and nurturing. A way of being that is in tune
with the individual will facilitate a sense of self, which will lead
naturally to individuation and independence.

From the outset, treatment needs to focus on empowering these
individuals, who are often caught in a victim frame of mind.
Even if we adopt a stepped approach, we still need to ensure
that there are choices at each stage to suit each individual's
needs and that the entrance to treatment is relatively quick.
Sometimes there is only a small window of clarity, and so

opportunity to change, in the repeated cycle of drinking or drug use.

Current treatment practices often reflect the different stages of the Cycle of Change as it relates to the recovery process but current treatment stops short of resolving the underlying issues and as a result of this too many individuals repeat treatment many times.

I believe that healing can only be achieved by;

1. the establishment of a strong sense of self,

2. the re-integration of the body/mind split,

3. the replacing of a cruel internalised voice by a kind, nurturing one,

4. allowing dependency issues to be resolved, and

5. processing the original trauma(s).

What is being proposed above is no different from any other model of counselling for helping individuals who are experiencing emotional distress and have little sense of self. People who use substances are exactly that, no different, once the substance is taken out of the equation.

Psychotherapy theory suggests that what is needed is a continuous, long-term, reparative relationship with one person who can perform the function of the good-enough mother, rather than short bursts of treatment or a care pathway that involves many different agencies. My experience as a psychotherapist suggests that eighteen months is the minimum amount of counselling sufficient to give an individual a strong enough sense of self for them to move on. Different agencies might well be necessary for many individuals, but this long-term one-to-one work could run alongside current practice and continue after the rehabilitation work has been completed.

Psychotherapy theory has much to offer in terms of how professionals working with addicted individuals can work in many different ways. How we perceive the underlying causes of addiction will impact on how we understand the function of addiction, how we assess the individual's mind-set and behaviour, how we view recovery, how we best structure our treatment plan and most crucially, how we are with those individuals. In addition, these theories are also useful for anyone living with an addiction. The understanding allows us to become both more self-compassionate and empathic and compassionate to others.

I hope that this small volume presents a case for all practitioners working in the addictions field or become aware of psychotherapy theory, primarily as it relates to good-enough mothering, container-contained, disillusionment, a coherent sense of self, shame and the mind/body split. I hope that these understandings elicit increased compassion from practitioners, family members and anyone using drink or drugs to self soothe. I hope to have made a case for offering relatively long-term counselling or psychotherapy to anyone in recovery. Finally, if nothing else, I hope I have opened the door to an opportunity for a discussion of these issues.

Further reading:

KAHN M. (2001) *Between Therapist and Client.* NY: Henry Holt and Co.

KEPNER J.I. (1996) *Healing Tasks - Psychotherapy with Adult Survivors of Childhood Abuse.* Cambridge. MA: Gestalt Press.

REFERENCES

ARNOLD L. (1995) *Women and Self-Injury – A Survey of 76 women.* Bristol Crisis Service for Women, PO Box 654, Bristol BS99 1XH.

BATEMAN A. & HOLMES J. (1995) *Introduction to Psychoanalysis.* London: Routledge.

BELL D. (1998) External injury and the internal world. In *C. Garland (Ed.) Understanding trauma: A Psychoanalytical Approach.* London: Duckworth.

BERNE E (1961) *Transactional Analysis in Psychotherapy.* N.Y.: Grove Press

BERNE E (1970) *The Games People Play.* London: Penguin Books

BERNHARDT P, BENTZEN M & ISAACS J (1995) Waking The Body Ego: Lisbeth Marcher's Somatic Developmental Psychology, Parts 1. In *Energy and Character, 26 (1), pp 47-54.*

BION W.R. (1962) *Learning from Experience.* London: Heinemann.

BEISSER A. (1970) The Paradoxical Theory of Change. In *Gestalt Theory Now.* Edited by Fagan J. and Shepherd I.L.

BRITTON R. (1992) Keeping things in mind. In *Clinical Lectures on Klein and Bion. Edited by R. Anderson London: Routledge.*

CASHDAN S. (1988) *Object Relations Therapy – Using the Relationship.* New York; W.W. Norton & Company Inc.

CARROLL R. (2002) Biodynamic Massage in Psychotherapy: Re-integrating, re-owning and re-associating through the body. In *Body Psychotherapy edited by Tree Staunton*

CLARKSON P. (1989) *Gestalt Counselling in Action.* London: Sage Publications.

CLARKSON P. (1995) *The Therapeutic Relationship.* London: Whurr Publishers

CLARKSON P. (2002) *The Transpersonal Relationship in Psychotherapy.* London: Whurr Publishers THE DIANOSTIC CRITERIA FROM DSM-IV (2 American Psychiatric Association. Washington, DC

ERSKINE R.G. (1995) A Gestalt Theory Approach to Shame and Self-Righteousness: Theory and Methods. In *British Gestalt Journal,* 4, pp107-117.

EVANS K. (1994) Healing Shame: A Gestalt Perspective. In *Transactional Journal Vol. 24, No. 2, April 1994, pp103-107.*

FRAIBERG S. (1982) Pathological Defenses in Infancy. In *Psychoanalysis Quarterly,* **51,** p. 612-635.

FREUD S. (1912) Recommendations to physicians practicing psychoanalysis pp.109-120 in *The Standard Edition vol. 12. London: Hogarth Press.*

FREUD S. (1926) Inhibitions, Symptoms and Anxiety. In *Freud Library Vol. 10.* London: Penguin.

FREUD S. (1933) New Introductory Lectures on Psycho-Analysis. In *Standard Edition Vol. 22*. London: Hogarth Press

GELSO C. J. & CARTER J. A. (1985) The relationship in Counseling and Psychotherapy: Components, consequences, and theoretical antecedents. In *The Counseling Psychologist, 41 (3), 296-306.*

GENDLIN E. (1996) *Focusing Orientated Psychotherapy*. London: The Guildford Press.

GERHARDT S. (2004) *Why Love Matters – How affection shapes a baby's brain*. London: Routledge

GILBERT P. (2001) Evolutionary approaches to psychopathology: the role of natural defences. In *Australian and New Zealand Journal of Psychiatry*. vol. 35, pp 17-27.

GILBERT P. & Compassionate Mind training for people with high PROCTER S. (2005) shame and self-criticism: Overview and pilot study of a group therapy approach. Submitted to *Clinical Psychology and Psychotherapy on 22.8.2005*

GILBERT P & MILES J.N.V. (2000) Sensitivity to put-down: Its relationship to perceptions of shame, social anxiety, depression, anger and self-other blame. In *Personality and Individual Differences*, Vol. 29, pp 757-774.

GRAY A. (1994) *An Introduction to the Therapeutic Frame*. London: Routledge.

GRIFFIN J. & TYRELL I, (2003) *Human Givens. A new approach to emotional health and clear thinking*. Chalvington, UK: HG Publishing Ltd.

GUGGENBUHL-CRAIG A (1971) Power in the Helping Professions. Dallas, Texas: Spring

HARRIS T. (1995) *I'm OK – You're OK.* Reading: Arrow Books

HAWKINS P & SHOHET R (2000) *Supervision in the Helping Professions.* Buckingham: Open University Press.

HEIMANN P. (1950) On Counter-transference. In *International Journal of Psycho-Analysis.* 31, pp.81-84.

HOFER M.A. (1994) Early relationships as regulators of infant physiology and behaviour. In *Acta Pardiatrica,* 397, pp 9-18.

HOLLIS J (1998) *The Eden Project. In Search of the Magical Other. A Jungian Perspective on Relationship.* Toronto: Inner City Books.

HYATT WILLIAMS A. (2003) Container and Contained: the school of Bion. In *The Psychodynamics of Addiction.* Edited by Martin Weegmann & Robert Cohen.

JACOBS M. (1986) *The Presenting Past.* Buckingham: Open University Press.

JOYCE P. & C. SILLS (2001) *Skills in Gestalt Counselling and Psychotherapy.* London: Sage

KAHN M. (2001) *Between Therapist and Client.* NY: Henry Holt and Co.

KARPMAN S. (1968) Fairy Tales and Script Drama Analysis. In *Transactional Analysis Bulletin, vol. 7, no. 26, pp. 39-43.*

KAUFMANN (1985) *Shame: the power of caring.* Cambridge, Mass: Schenkman Books.

KELEMAN S. (1981) *Your body speaks its mind.* Berkeley, CA: Center Press Lt.

KEPNER J.I. (1996) *Healing Tasks – Psychotherapy with Adult Survivors of Childhood Abuse*. Cambridge. MA: Gestalt Press.

KEPNER J.I. (1987) *Body Process – Working with Body in Psychotherapy*. San Francisco: Jossey Bass Publishers.

KLEIN M. (1946) Some notes on Schizoid Mechanisms. In *Envy and Gratitude and Other Works 1946-1963*. London: Vintage 1997.

KLEIN M. (1952) Some Theoretical Conclusions Regarding the Emotional Life of the Infant in *Envy and Gratitude and Other Works 1946-1963*. London : Vintage 1997.

KLEIN M. (1963) On the sense of Loneliness. In *Envy and Gratitude and Other Works 1946-1963*. London: Vintage 1997.

KOHUT H. (1971) *The Analysis of Self*. New York: International Universities Press.

LITTLE M. (1951) Counter-transference and the Patient's Response to it. In *International Journal of Psychoanalysis*. **32**, pp32-40.

MACKEWN J. (1997) *Developing Gestalt Counselling*. London: Sage

MAIN M. (1994) A Move to the Level of Representation In The Study of Attachment Organisation: Implications for Psychoanalysis. *Annual Research Lecture to the British Psychoanalytical Society: London 6.7.1994*

MILLER W.R. & S. ROLLNICK (1991) *Motivational Interviewing*. NY: Guildford Press

MILLER B.A., DOWNS W.R. & TESTA M. (1993). Interrelationships between victimization experiences and women's alcohol use. *Journal of Studies on Alcohol* 11. pp 109-117.

MULLEN P.E. & FLEMING J. (1998) Long-term Effects of Child *Sexual Abuse* Issues in *Child Abuse Prevention*

NATHANSON D.L. (1992) *Shame and Pride. Affect, Sex and the Birth of the Self.* New York: W.W. Norton & Co. Ltd

PARLETT M. and HEMMINGS J. (1990) *Gestalt Therapy in Handbook of Individual Therapy* edited by Windy Dryden. London: Sage

PERLS F, HEFFERLINE R.F. & GOODMAN P. (1984) *Gestalt Therapy.* London:Sovenir Press

PERRY B.D., POLLARD R.A., BLAKLEY T.L, BAKER W L & VIGILANTE D. (1995) Childhood Trauma, the neurobiology of adaptation and "use-dependent" development of the brain: How "states" become "traits". In *Infant Mental Health Journal*, 16, pp271-291.

PROCHASKA J.O. & DICLEMENTE C.C. & NORCROSS J.C. (1992) In search of how people change. Applications to addictive behaviors. In *American Psychologist.* 47, (9) pp1102-1114.

REICH W. (1947) *The Function of the Orgasm.* Reprinted in Souvenir Press 1983.

ROGERS, C.R. (1951) *Client Centred Therapy.* London: Constable

ROGERS C.R. (1959) A Theory of Therapy, Personality and Interpersonal Relationships. In Kock, S (Ed) Psychology: A Study of Science.

ROTHSCHLD B. (2002) Body Psychotherapy without touch: applications for trauma therapy. In *Body Psychotherapy edited by Tree Staunton*

RUMI *The Essential Rumi*. Translated by Colman Barks (1995). London: Penguin Books.

RYCROFT C. (1995) *The Critical Dictionary of Psychoanalysis.* London: Penguin

SACRET J. (1999) Interrelationships between internal and external factors in early development: current Kleinian thinking and implications for technique. In *Psychoanalytic Psychotherapy in the Kleinian Tradition.* Edited by Ruszczynski S. and Johnson S.

SCHORE A. (1994) *Affect regulation and the origin of the self: the neurobiology of emotional development.* Hillsdale: Erlbaum.

SCHORE A. (2001) The Effects of Early Relational Trauma on Right Brain Development, Affect Regulation, and Infant Mental Health.' *Infant Mental Health Journal.* Volume 22, 1,pp 201-269.

STERN D.N. (1998) *The Interpersonal World of the Infant.* London: Karnac Books.

STEWART I. (1989) *Transactional Analysis Counselling in Action.* London: Sage

STREAN H. (1985) *Therapeutic Principles in Practice.* California: Sage

TOMKINS S. S (1963), *Affect, Imagery, Consciousness.* Volume 2. NY: Springer.

TOTTEN N. & EDMONDSON (1988) *Reichian Growth Work.* Bridport: Prism Press.

TURP M. (2001) Psychosomatic Health – The body and the Word. Basingstoke: Palgrave.

TURP M. (2003) *Hidden self-harm. Narratives from Psychotherapy.* London: Jessica Kingsley Publishers Ltd.

VELLEMAN R. (1992) *Counselling for Alcohol Problems.* London: Sage.

WHELTON W.J & GREENBERG L.S. (2005) Emotion in self-criticism. In *Personality and Individual Differences*, Volume 38, pp 1583-1585.

WIDOM, C.S. (1993) Child abuse and alcohol use and abuse. In: Martin, S.E.; ed., *Alcohol and Interpersonal Violence: Fostering Multidisciplinary Perspectives.* NIAAA Research Monograph No. 24. NIH Publication No. 93-3496. Bethesda, MD: National Institute on Alcohol Abuse and Alcoholism, pp 291-314.

WILSNACK, S.C., VOGELTANZ N.D, KLASSEN A.D& HARRIS, T.R. (1997) Childhood sexual abuse and women's substance abuse: National survey findings. In *Journal of Studies on Alcohol* 58(3): 264-271.

WINNICOTT D.W. (1949) 'Mind and its relation to the Psyche-Soma.' In *Collected Papers Through Paediatrics to Psychoanalysis.* London:Tavistock, 1958.

WINNICOTT D.W. (1956) 'Primary Maternal Preoccupation.' In *Collected Papers Through Paediatrics to Psychoanalysis.* London:Tavistock, 1958.

WINNICOTT D.W. (1960) Ego Distortion in Terms of True and False Self in *The Maturational Processes and the Facilitating Environment.* London: Hogarth, 1965.

WINNICOTT D.W. (1960) 'The Theory of the Parent-Infant

Relationship.' In *The Maturational Processes and the Facilitating Environment.* London: Hogarth, 1965.

WINNICOTT D.W. (1988) *Babies and their mothers.* London: Free Books Association.

WURMER L, (1981) *The Mask of Shame.* Baltimore: John Hopkins University Press.

YONTEF G. M. (1993) *Awareness, dialogue and process.* New York: The Gestalt Journal Press, Inc.

INDEX

A

Abstinence 62, 73, 79–81, 119, 132, 136, 138, 142, 150–151

Abstinence - enforced 80

Abuse xi, xvi, xvii, 1–3, 13–15, 42, 45, 49, 67, 84, 92, 94, 148, 151, 153, 159–160, 162

Action xvii, xix, 14, 23, 28–29, 42, 60–61, 66–68, 73–74, 77, 80, 83, 85, 98, 121, 125–126, 132, 134, 138, 143, 148–150, 156, 161

Adult xix, 12, 14–15, 26, 33, 69, 85, 94, 116, 130, 153, 159

Alcoholics Anonymous xvi

Anger 15, 19–22, 34, 44, 48, 51, 67–69, 71, 87, 93, 95–96, 98, 102–103, 106, 111, 116, 121, 130, 132, 146, 157

Arnold 3, 155

B

Bateman & Holmes xxi, 36, 49, 155

Beisser 81, 155

Bell 13, 155

Berne xx, 37, 42, 49, 155

Bernhardt 55, 155

Bessel van Kolk et al 84

Bion xx, 25–26, 155–156, 158

Blank screen xvi–xvii, 148

Body armouring. 52

Body memory 54, 60–61, 97

Body posture. 51

Boundaries 21, 28, 128, 143

Breath 51–52, 93, 131

Breathing exercises 53, 56

Breathing rhythm xxi

Britton 35, 156

C

Care pathway 152

CASHA 2, 7, 11

Cashdan 133, 156

Cause and effect 4, 14, 32

Chemical detox 143

Child   xix, 12–14, 18, 20–21, 26–28, 30–31, 34, 41, 61, 65–66, 68, 72, 79, 82, 85, 93–94, 98, 103–104, 116–117, 137, 145, 151, 160, 162

Clarkson xviii, 85, 129, 147, 156

Co-dependency 22, 150

Compassion xi–xii, xiv, 9, 15–16, 42, 153

Compulsion to repeat 71–72

Confluence 68, 128–129

Container xx, 26, 34, 123, 153, 158

Containment 25–26, 30–32, 34–35, 144, 150–151

Contemplation 73–74, 110, 123–124, 132, 135

Continuum model of self-harm 2

Counselling xvi, xix, xxi, 17, 20, 23, 57, 63, 76, 82, 85, 105–106, 109, 113, 139, 141–142, 144, 145, 149, 152–153, 156, 158–159, 161–162

Cravings 61–62

Creative adjustment 121, 129

Culturally accepted self-harming acts 2

D

Davies and Frawley 18

Denial 8, 20, 39–42, 51, 73, 81, 95, 111, 113–114, 121, 126, 136–137, 146

Dependency 6, 22, 110, 118, 136–137, 150, 152

Depressive position 37–38, 41, 44

Dissociation 15, 18

Drama Triangle 42, 44, 46–47, 91–92, 94, 117, 127

Dynamic iv, 42, 44, 47–49, 80, 96, 117, 128–129, 133

E

Ego-destructive superego 35

Ego state. 13

Emotional distress – intensity 7, 16, 20, 22, 26, 55, 62, 77

Emotions - suppressed 19, 21, 22, 67, 87, 95

Emotions - transitory nature 30

Emotion - unacceptable 20–21, 67

Erskine 68, 70, 72, 130, 156

Evans 70, 79, 156

F

False Self 121, 162

Favazza 1

Fear system 16, 23, 37, 39, 59, 143

Felt sense 7, 57–59, 66, 80, 149

Fight- flight response 39

Focusing 40, 56–57, 64, 128, 138, 149, 157

Fraiberg 130, 156

Frame of mind 12, 15, 42, 47, 106, 151

Frank 147

Freud xvi, 71, 156–157

G

Gelso and Carter xviii

Gendlin 57, 64, 157

Genetic make-up 25

Gerhardt 31, 157

Gilbert xx, 15, 40, 49, 157

Gilbert and Miles 15

Gilbert and Proctor xx

Goal 42, 66, 73–74, 77, 79–80, 122, 132, 148–149

Good-enough mother 25, 28, 35, 152

Guggenbuhl-Craig 49, 157

Guilt 19, 34, 38, 77, 104, 121, 133

H

Hawkins and Shohet 49

Hill 147

Historical self 144, 149

Holding 7, 25–26, 29, 39, 51–52, 65, 82, 119, 126

Humanistic psychotherapy xviii, xix

Humiliation 68, 71, 84

Hynan 147

I

Idealization 112

Immediate gratification 23

Impact on another xvii, 68, 132

Independence. 136, 146, 151

Individuation 151

Internalise authority figures 15

Intrinsic shame 78–79

J

Jacobs 23, 27, 158

K

Kahn xxi, 153, 158

Karpman xx, 37, 42, 50, 158

Kaufmann 69, 83, 85, 158

Kepner 18, 55, 64, 153, 159

Kohut 66, 159

L

Lapse 5–6, 12, 42, 58, 66, 72–75, 76–81, 102, 150

Librium 143

Loss 60, 103, 114, 121, 126, 138, 145–146

Luborsky 147

M

MacKewn 128

Main xvi, 35, 40, 54, 83, 89–90, 114, 117, 131, 134, 159

Maintenance 63, 73, 109–110

Massage 53, 55–56, 60, 63, 156

Melanie Klein xiv, xx, 37, 133

Mental health 148, 160–161

Mind/ body xvii, xxi, 54, 57, 59, 61, 70, 80, 96, 145, 149–150, 152

Mirroring 66

Motivational interviewing 142, 159

N

Narrative xiii, xxi, 9, 28, 32, 47, 87, 95–96, 111, 115, 119, 125, 129, 130, 134, 149, 162

Neural pathways 31, 35

Neuroscience 31

O

Ogden 127

P

Paradoxical theory of change 81, 155

Paranoia 16, 39, 54

Paranoid-schizoid position 37–39, 41, 44

Parent xix, 12–15, 18–19, 21–22, 34, 36, 40, 42, 66, 69, 71, 82, 90–91, 94, 97, 99, 112, 116–120, 122, 124, 128–129, 131–133, 137–138, 162

Perception xviii, 2, 16, 33, 38–39, 41, 47, 118, 120, 124, 144, 157

Perry et al 35

Persecutory anxiety 38, 44

Personal development 144

Person-centred xix, 147

Physical contact 26, 28, 60, 69, 147

Pre-contemplation 73, 124

Prochaska, Diclemente and Norcross 72

Pseudo-independent 136

Psychic fantasies 38

Psychological contact 28, 69

Psychotherapy xii–xiii, xvi–xviii, xix, xxi, 9, 26, 34, 64, 113, 141–142, 152–153, 155–162

Q

Qualitative leap model of self-harm 2

Quick fix 23, 73

R

Reich xx, 52, 160

Reiki 56, 63

Relapse prevention 142, 144

Relaxation techniques 144

Reparative relationship xviii, xxi, 28, 81, 85, 148, 152

Rescuer 43–44, 46–48, 91, 94, 117–118

Research xvii, 3, 15, 31, 147, 159, 162

Rogers 56, 147, 160

Roles 42, 44–47, 90

Rothschild 60

S

Sacret 31, 34, 161

Schore 31, 161

Self as an evolving entity 144

Self-compassion xii, 15

Self-criticism 15–16, 69, 157, 162

Self-disclosure 130

Self esteem 4

Self-harm vii, xiii, xix, 1–9, 17, 35, 70, 141, 162
Self-harm – definition 1–2
Self-hate 15
Self-soothe 8, 14–15, 17, 20, 30, 34–36, 39, 63, 77, 146
Self worth 68
Shame - antidote 73
Shame – defences against 83–84
Shame - issues underlying 67
Shame - language 78, 83
Shame - process 15
Shame – repeating cycle 72
Skin boundary 26, 53, 56, 60, 63
Social isolation 87, 94
Splitting 38–39, 41–42, 133
Stean 118
Stewart 12, 23, 161
Stress 4–5, 12, 15–16, 28, 39, 40, 90, 126, 143
Stress continuum 12
Supervision. 49
Sustainable recovery. 149

T

The "bad" mother 37
The Cycle of Change 72, 74, 76, 78, 109, 123, 132, 138, 142, 152
The "good" mother 37
The 'I' 70
The inter-personal bridge 69

The 'me'.. 60, 70
The Parent/Adult/Child model xix
Threat 16, 23, 35, 39–40, 53
Tomkins 21, 161
Totten and Edmondson 51, 67
Transactional Analysis xix, 12, 23, 50, 155, 158, 161
Transference xvi, xvii, xix, xx, 12, 110, 118–121, 128–129, 132, 145, 148, 158, 159
Transference relationship xvi–xvii
Trauma 12, 17–18, 72, 84, 149, 152, 155, 160–161
Trauma - effect 13, 34, 52
Treatment xvi, xix, 42, 58, 78, 85, 87, 141–144, 151–153
Treatment plan 153
Treatment - stepped approach 142, 151
Turp xix, 1–3, 6–7, 9, 162

U

Unconscious fantasies 38, 133
Unfinished business. 72, 120

V

Verbal narrative 32
Victim xvii, xx, 42–46, 78, 82, 84, 92, 117–118, 127, 148, 151

W

Wanigaratne and Keaney 141
Weegmann 4, 158

Whelton and Greenberg 15

Winnicott xx, 25–27, 36, 118, 121, 162–163

Wurmser 67

Y

Yontef 77, 79, 163

Printed in Great Britain
by Amazon